"Whoever does not remember the lessons of history is
doomed to repeat them"

Mayrbek TARAMOV

Russia's Crimes of the Century in Chechnya

Dedicated to the memory of Natalya Estemirova, Aset Mazhaeva and other the murdered activists of the Human Rights Centre „Memorial", who put to paper many witness statements and took photographs.

© Copyright by Mayrbek Taramov, 2015

Photo Credit by Natalia Medvedeva
©MELNIKOFF Galleries Network

Photo © Vladimir Mashatin
© Photocopyright belongs to the newspaper and website
«Caucasian Herald» www.kvestnik.org
©www.chechenpress.com

Cover design Mayrbek Taramov
Layout Elena Maglevannaya
Reviewer – Akhmed Zakaev, Vice-Prime-minister Chechen Republic of Ichkeria.
Editor – Mayrbek Taramov.
Translator – Masha Karp

Under the cover of a glib phrase „the anti-terrorist operation" monstrous murders of peaceful citizens were organized in Chechnya. At the very beginning of the war on 21st October 1999 the heavily populated areas of the capital Grozny and other residential areas of Chechnya were attacked by tactical missiles of the Tochka U „ground to ground" type. And when the people fled for their lives and rushed into „humanitarian corridors" kindly provided by the Russian leadership the wretched refugees were cold-bloodedly shot at from all kinds of weapons.
Everything that the Russian army did in Chechnya and the Russian special services continue doing there now falls under the definition of state terrorism and the Russian leadership should be severely punished for that.
Let this book be an indictment for the future trial of the Russian criminals.

Table of Contents

Akhmed Zakaev: „Cruelty and Insidiousness Unheard of in History!"..4

Missile Strike on the centre of Grozny and other residential areas of the Chechen Republic...6

Bombardment of the „humanitarian corridor" on 29 October 1999 on the Moscow-Baku Highway at the border with the Republic of Ingushetia...53

Execution of "humanitarian corridor 2" on the way to Dagestan on October 29, 1999...69

Russian Cadaverology..103

PS. A letter from the Nazran office of Memorial to the editor of the website „Kavkazsky Vestnik"..124

Facts Warning the World...126

Conclusion..132

Reviews..133

Akhmed Zakaev: „Cruelty and Insidiousness Unheard of in History!"

Instead of a preface

I, Akhmed Zakaev, can testify that all the awful facts described in this book did really take place during the latest Chechen war as at that time I was the First Vice Prime Minister and was in the Chechen Republic side by side with its President Aslan Maskhadov.

Studying the missile-bomb and artillery strikes of the Chechen residential areas I came to the firm conclusion that this was a deliberate action of the Russian military forces aimed at mass extermination of the Chechen peaceful population. This is confirmed by the testimonies of victims and eye-witnesses, journalists and human rights activists. These murderous actions had yet another goal – they tried to push those who remained alive into Russia in order to persecute them there – all over the vast country and then assimilate the rest. That was the way to stop the Chechens existing as a nation.

The Russian leadership worked to prepare the world public opinion for the acknowledgement of the fact that after the actions of the Russian militarists, the people, who stayed in Chechnya, would be without exception labelled terrorists and bandits, who do not deserve any mercy and should all be exterminated. And if they are „terrorists", according to the new anti-terrorist mandate, no international norms or conventions, which usually apply to combatants, i.e. participants of usual military operations, should be applied to them Unfortunately, this is what happened – the world community, duped by the Kremlin-Lubyanka propaganda, believed nearly every word of Russia's young and energetic leader – Vladimir Putin.

It took four years of bloodshed before the horrible shocking scale of these lies came to the surface. It happened thanks to honest and courageous journalists and human rights activists. I would like to single out those working for the Human Rights Centre „Memorial", who were involved in strenuous and extremely dangerous work. I can only bow low to their courage. Thank you!

As far as I can see it, the Russian military leadership started methodical and systematic bombardment and shelling along the whole perimeter of the republic trying to drive the biggest number of refugees into the capital Grozny and only then delivered a strike by tactical missiles straight into the centre of this heavily populated city. But even this was not the most insidious blow. The epitome of the insidiousness and cynicism was the strike delivered on the exhausted refugees, who thought that their salvation was a footstep away in the humanitarian corridors. Poor people! They hoped that they would be given a chance to leave the republic that was being shelled. But having gathered all these refugees in one spot, the Russians carried out a genocide. Such insidiousness, cynicism and cruelty towards peaceful citizens have not been seen in history. This happened on the eve of the new, third millennium. This is how the humankind entered a new century.

Reading this book will make you shudder – its pages are saturated with blood of innocent people. Nobody should ever forget this! Those who are guilty of this horrible ruthless crime, „the Crime of the Century" as it was dubbed, should be severely punished. In the first place, I mean Putin, Yeltsin, Patrushev, Sergei Ivanov, Gryzlov, Shamanov, Troshev – everybody who was involved in the Chechen genocide. And it is not that I am being bloodthirsty – not at all, but it is important to prevent crimes like this from happening again. (And yet in 2008, several years after the episode that has just been described, exactly when the book was for the first time being translated into English, Shamanov – the cruellest of all Russian generals – was received and entertained with much kindness by President Bush in the White House. – *Ed.*) And then suddenly, instead of being punished, the Russian criminals called for my extradition – they wanted to get me, the man, who together with other fighters of the Chechen resistance opposed heinous crimes of Russian military and political leadership.

Oh, Almighty Allah! How should this be called? How has it become possible? Is there any limit to the hideous lies, insidiousness and hypocrisy of the Russian leadership? How could this have happened that tomorrow, 13th November I'll have to appear before the British court where the issue of my extradition to Russia will be decided, the extradition to the country, which devours my fellow countrymen by day and by night? The trial tomorrow should put a full stop in my drawn- out case. I am sure that the wise British justice will return its fair verdict. Moreover, I think that not only the UK court and the British public will side with me, but all the people of good will, who would like to have the one and only inviolable truth. I am sure that the international com- munity should finally condemn the Russian leadership, which turned lawlessness and tyranny into law – it has become especially noticeable in relations to the events happening in Russia.

As Alexander Litvinenko, a genuine patriot of Russia and Chechnya once said, I very much hope that the day will come when Russian and Chechen peoples will bring Putin, Yeltsin and all the political and military leadership of Russia to trial and this trial will take place in the middle of Grozny, which used to be the most beautiful city in the Caucuses and which has been left in ruins by the contemporary Russian barbarians.

Akhmed Zakaev, First Vice Prime Minister of the Chechen Republic of Ichkeria, London, 12-11-2003

Missile Strike on the centre of Grozny and other residential areas of the Chechen Republic

Instead of an epigraph:

The Prime Minister Putin reports to the President Yeltsin: Yesterday our battle-planes bombed the terrorist targets in Chechnya. Several training facilities and storage structures of terrorists were destroyed.
Yeltsin: Give me more detail...
Putin: Two schools, a university, a factory, two hospitals, a maternity hospital.
Yeltsin: Why? Was everybody there a terrorist?
Putin: Yes sir! Secondary schools prepared ordinary terrorists, universities prepared professionals. In hospitals terrorists were treated and recuperated, at the factories they worked , in the maternity hospitals they were born.
Yeltsin: That means the whole republic is solidly inhabited by terrorists. So we are doing the right thing to bomb them, aren't we?

Mayrbek Taramov, „The Caucasians Herald" newspaper 15th October 1999

A Report of the Information Centre of the Operations Directorate of the ChRI Military Forces

In the evening of 21St October 1999 at about 5pm the Russian barbarians attacked the most densely populated areas of Grozny with tactical „ground to ground" missiles: the Central Maternity Hospital, the Central Market, the Olympics district, the Central Post-Office and the Mosque of Kalinin settlement at the time of the evening namaz. At the moment 68 bodies have been identified in the area of the Central Market. In Kalinin settlement, in the Mosque and in the Olympics district the Russian-made rockets killed 41 and wounded 112 people. In the Central Maternity Hospital 28 people died and 95 were wounded – most of them women and children.

According to the data received on the day the total number of casualties of the missile attack was 137 people dead and 260 wounded.

The ChRI leadership was going to make an official statement about the incident.

„Caucasians Herald" newspaper, №16 1st November 1999

„A tube appeared in the air and a ball came out of it, red as the sun at sunset"

(Malika Yunusova's statement, Human Rights Centre „Memorial")
My husband and I had been trading – mostly selling food – at Grozny Central Market since 1996. Our stall was next to „the exchange" (currency exchange point– *Ed.*). I have four children, their ages ranging from 5 to 14. On that day, the 21st October, early in the morning we were at the market as usual. There were plenty of people as it had been before the war. Before that day Katayama settlement and the traffic police checkpoint had already been attacked by depth-bombs.

On 18th October I sent my children off to the village of Kotar-Yurt. It was an ordinary day. My husband went home for the afternoon prayer. This was Thursday. We wanted to go and visit the children on that evening. When my husband came back from his prayer he told me that he had dozed off and had a dream about his late cousin. My husband was scared and said that it was a bad omen. I replied that we would go to Kotar-Yurt to see the family, I wanted to calm him down. We did not think that something might happen to us. My husband was hurrying me up, he kept saying: „Get ready, let's get going!"

I used to take a portable oven with me to the market, it ran on petrol. I cooked a meal so that we could leave for home in the evening. We ate. My husband and his friend went to „the exchange" that was behind me. He told me to get ready and stepped aside.

At about 4.30 I heard some noise, the sound was like din in my ears. I wasn't even frightened. It was not like thunder, just something incomprehensible. Then there was silence. Then a tube appeared in the air and a ball came out of it, red as the sun at sunset. And it burst in front of my eyes. And then there was a terrible roar, like a strong thunder. I got scared, it deafened me. I did not remember all this before – for about five months I had a partial loss of memory.

The tube fell straight down on „the exchange". And the ball that burst turned into shrapnel within a second – this was at the time when people were starting to leave the market. It lasted just a second and as a result of it people were without heads, without arms, without legs, with their tummies torn out. I could not hear anything, I just saw it with my eyes. I could not help anybody – my right arm was fractured. It was impossible to help anybody. Just everybody who was there – those who were passing by, who were standing about, who were trading – just everybody was now down. One person fell over another. Three people were lying over my husband. They were dead, but he was alive.

I could not hear any shouting or groaning, I saw mouths opening, people making pain grimaces. People who were barely alive moved with difficulty and fell down at once. I took my wounded arm with my hand, moved away from the table, went to the other side of the table and ran. I was looking for my husband and could not find him. I was simply looking for the jacket he was wearing. I walked for about 20 meters. I was walking over dead bodies, slipped, fell down and was rolling in the blood there. I fell down, got up and just about 5 meters from my table I saw my husband in his leather jacket lying here. I came up to him, touched him, shook him, he looked at me. We both understood that we were alive. We spoke as dumb people – neither he nor myself could hear a thing. He embraced me with both arms – he had not been hurt. And the people who pushed my husband away (there were two men and a woman) were torn to pieces. He caught my arm – it hurt so. I thought I did not have any arm any more. We ran, and did not know where we were running. The market was near tramlines. We lived near the stop called „Zavodskaya". Our neighbour came running. When he heard what had happened he ran towards the market. He met us, got a car and even at this time some pieces of shrapnel were still flying around. At Zavodskaya stop there was a yellow bus. I was taken to the hospital by the same car. It was evening. There were no lights and the bus was following us. When we got to hospital number 9, this bus was fully packed (only one woman, a little boy and a driver, who was barely alive, got out of there by themselves), other people were then taken out, but all of them were dead. The bus was standing at the bus-stop, but all the people inside were dead. I saw it with my own eyes. I forgot about myself. These people were dragged out and laid on the stairs of hospital № 9. The hospital was fully packed – the corridors, the stairs. Doctors there did not know where to start, who to take inside, who to help. They said: „Don't wait here, take them away, we don't have vacant beds". People died within half an hour (from the blood loss – *Ed*).

Then I was taken to the Central Republican Hospital. I managed to get there before the influx of people. They took shrapnel out of my arm „live" (without anesthetics – *Ed*). Then people started coming. When it was necessary they switched on the light. I lost count to the people who died there. In the morning a plane bombardment started. My family came to pick me up at 6 am. People kept coming and the hospital kept operating till dawn. I was told that I would be taken to Nazran, but the roads were blocked. I was taken home. Then again by car I was taken to the hospital in Achhoy-Martan (they hid me from check-points as patrols were checking inside the cars. They thought that all the wounded were militants and snipers). I was given treatment in Achhoy-Martan.

I had a neighbour in Kotar-Yurt. She used to trade next to me – her name was Raisa. She had 6 children and she was pregnant with the seventh After the attack on the market she died.

People of the world, stand up for a minute!

(From the Notes of a Doctor Working for a Chechen village hospital)
– Where is my Mum? – a boy stops me as I am passing him by on the staircase landing.
– Who are you? – He answers in an unfamiliar language. He is neither Russian, nor Chechen, and I can't understand what ethnicity this is and there is no time to find out.

Whose boy is this one? Does anybody know?
There's silence and then a voice:
Maybe, it's the woman's who 's just been brought in and is now in the dressing room.

The woman is in a coma, she has lost a lot of blood. She has a shrapnel wound in her shoulder of her upper limb. The bone is crushed, and soft tissues survived only in a small area. The arm is hanging. The doctors are arguing, one says: „We have to amputate", the other finds her pulse and decides to sew it on. They feel sorry for her. She is a woman after all.

In the dressing room there is a table and a couch. She is lying on the table. On the couch there is her savior. The man is about 45, he is wounded in the thigh of his lower limb. He is bleeding, but he asks to help her first, her case is much more serious. They are the first, who were wounded by the Scud missiles (a foreign name for the „ground- ground „ rockets), which burst over Grozny Central Market.

Later w found out that a woman was from Azerbaijan and she was a seller at the market and the man came to do some shopping. The man was heavily wounded but he crawled to his car and asked the people around to put somebody, who was heavily wounded, in his car. They chose her. Although he was bleeding he came in his car from Grozny to the village Starye Atagi and brought this wounded Azeri woman. We learnt all this later. They were the first wounded. In 10-15 minutes it all started... The wounded came so fast that we did not have time to bring them in. Cars came and went. There was not enough medical staff. There were not enough stretchers, beds, medicines, dressings, solutions, everything, everything.... One doctor was sent to meet the cars – he looked into each car, selected those who were heavily wounded and sent the rest further down to Chiri-Yurt, Shatoy etc.

This was a baptism by fire for our small district hospital with 22 beds on 21st October 1999. Two surgeons, anesthetist, trauma specialist (he was sitting at home in an armchair watching television and saw the nightmare that was happening in Grozny, so he just came from his Chishki village to help his colleagues), several nurses and nurses' aids and many, many people staying overnight and helping with anything that was needed. And so many young people who were ready to give their blood. We checked their blood type and rhesus in a hurry.

The Azeri woman's arm would not take on, so a month later it had to be amputated. And 2 or 3 weeks after that the woman passed away leaving three orphans – two girls and the boy I met at the staircase landing. They were taken in by a Chechen family before their relatives came to pick them up.

Every day new wounded came , but also some doctors from Grozny City hospitals number 9 and 4 and also some nursing staff. After the first Scud missile there came the second one which hit the shop „Luch". Then there was the bombardment of „ the humanitarian corridor" that was full of refugees, and also missile bomb strikes over everything that moves. How many people died on the spot, how many on the way to the hospital, how many in the hospital? You can't count them. You look at somebody, yes he is wounded, seems to be recovering, starts getting up, starts walking – and then suddenly severe deterioration, delirium, fever and death. Neither antibiotics, nor antipyretics worked. Doctors did not know what to do. And how many died without regaining consciousness?

How can I forget a nine-year old Batukaev, who had been having fever of 39,5-41 degrees and then died without regaining consciousness Even the strongest antibiotics could not help him. How can I forget a shrill laughter and tears of a young woman, who about a week after she came to us asked somebody to help her to get up and was told that both her legs were amputated? It transpired that she had got married just a few days before she was wounded.

How can I forget a beautiful young woman of 22-25 whose arm was amputated and she was later taken to Moscow without learning that her husband and two children had been killed? When she asked: „Why is my husband not coming?", she was told: „He is looking after the children and it is dangerous to come here".

Her story was as follows. She decided to take her family to the village where her parents lived in Chernorechye. Hardly had they come to the water reservoir, when they saw a plane. They ran out of the car hoping to hide somewhere. The husband got the girl and the boy aged 5 and 3 under his arms and ran shouting to her to hurry up. She was the only one out of four who survived.

They wanted to take a wounded young man out of the republic, but he died on the way. On the same night his wife gave birth to a boy.

A Russian stunt pilot was happy to use not one, but two rockets for one Chechen girl... This is how it happened. Three girl-friends decided to go to the river to get some water. When they nearly reached home and were at the gates, a plane started circling round them. Two friends managed to get inside, but the third one started calling them, saying: „Come out, they won't hurt us!" The plane circled twice, and after the third circle when the dust settled, there on the ground was the girl and two shell craters – on her right and on her left. And she died in the hospital without regaining consciousness. How many women, men? children lost their limbs? Here in Baku, the capital of Azerbaijan, I see our patients every now and again.

During the „mopping-up" at 7am federal troops took a wounded man out of the hospital and two days later he was found in the woodland belt hanging upside down on a piece of wire, which ran through his ankles. He had no eyes, no ears, he was skinned alive, his fingers were deformed and three ribs were missing...

I remember many young guys coming to the hospital unconscious. Our hospital was small with 22 beds only, but later we had to use two corridors, a boiler room and a kitchen in the school nearby and place those, who were recuperating, in the classrooms. As soon as a patient regained consciousness, those who could sit up performed an ablution with the building sand (it was brought in little bags and put under the beds). Those who could not sit up, stroked the walls with their hands – and in this way having performed the ablution performed the namaz. There were problems with everything – with water, with lighting. We made operations under the candle light, at best we had flashlights. We did have a power unit, but as soon as planes appeared we switched it off. When the new wounded came, these guys asked „please if we have the medicines you need, just take them and save these people".

And if they had to die these young men died with great dignity. If you listened to what their moving lips were saying, you would hear not appeals for help, but ayahs and suras from Koran. Let Allah accept their jihad. This is how Chechen children remembered the most frightening day of their lives – the shooting of „the humanitarian corridor" on the motorway Rostov-Baku, 29th October 1999.

This is a dirty war, we all know it. This is an extermination, a genocide of the Chechen people. The guys who are fighting are neither bandits nor terrorists – they are our brothers and sons and they are fighting for our land. And if somebody wants to organize an anti-terrorist operation, they should start with the Kremlin.

Tactical missiles „ground to ground" of Tochka U type with multiple warheads, which were meant to target Western imperialists, struck against the country's own citizens

The view of Grozny Central Market after the missile attack

st October 1999. The vertical poles - the only remainder of stalls and awnings - testify that the explosion of the warhead took place over the market.

A shrapnel took off half of the man's head as he was sitting in a car

Raisa Hamzaeva, who lost her left arm and left eye as a result of the explosion of „ground to ground" missile over Grozny Central Market on 21st October 1999

The missile carrier, which landed in the centre of the town of Argun ith the Chechen children who were the first to get there.

The missile carrier „ground to ground" with the inventory number No 9M79/III84445, which landed in the centre of the town of Argun – hundreds of people witnessed that

Over thirty people died during the carpet bombing of the Elistanzhi village on 7th October 1999, the majority of them were children.

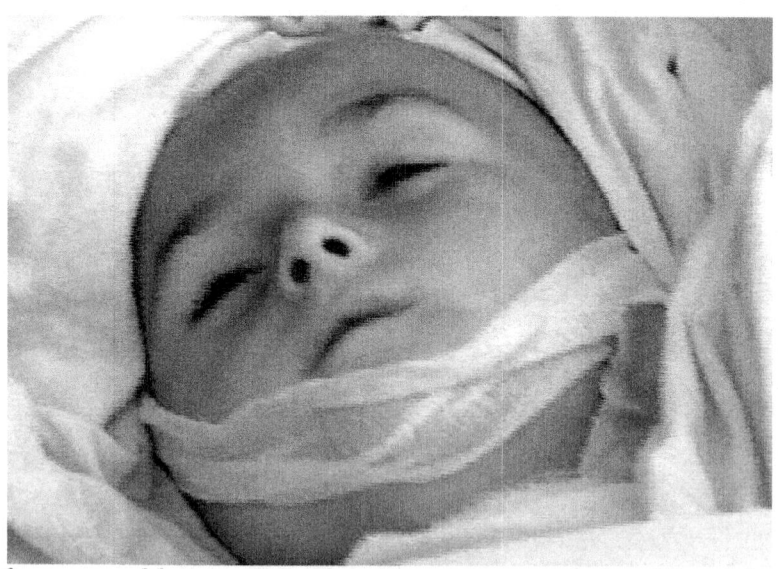

A four-year-old „terrorist" Adam Hamzatov – a victim of Russia's crime of the century and the Kremlin propaganda. The village of Elistanzhi, 7th October 1999

The bus, where the refugees of „the humanitarian corridor" were travelling, hit by the tank airburst projectile

The refugee transport was shot at point-blank from all kinds of weapons, although one can clearly see white „flags" made of sheets

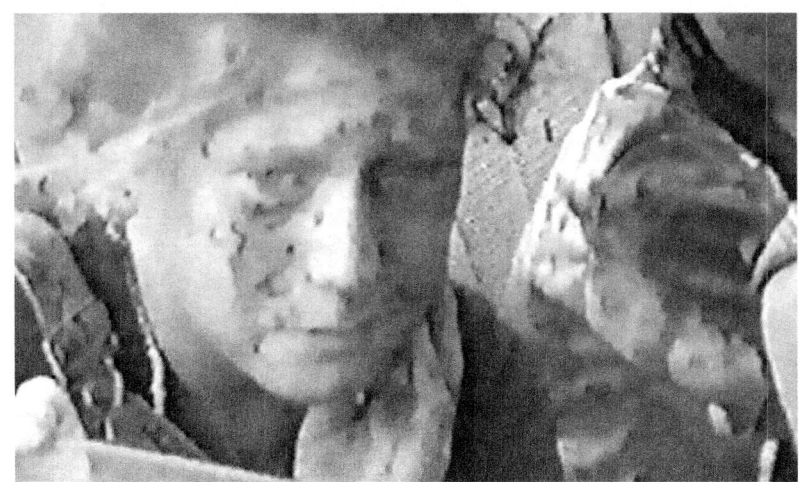

Children were the most vulnerable victims. After the bombardment of „the humanitarian corridor" on 29th October 1999

This is how Chechen children remembered the most frightening day of their lives – the shooting of „the humanitarian corridor" on the motorway Rostov-Baku, 29th October 1999

The refugee transport was shot at point-blank from all kinds of weapons, although one can clearly see white „flags" made of sheets. There are lots of organizations and groups aimed at protecting different kinds of animals. Some of them are put on the endangered species list – the Red Data Book. I would like to ask the world community: „If you think the Chechens are beasts, how many of us need to remain alive, for somebody to pay attention to us and put us on this list in the Red Data Book?
People, wake up! It might be too late tomorrow! You can be the next...

The wounded called me Yisha (sister). This is how I'll sign it: **Rosa Yisha**. *" The Caucasians Herald" newspaper. Written down by M. Taramov.*

„Leave Me. Just Let Me Die!"

(Testimony of Zelimhan Gireyev about the missile strike on Grozny Central Market, 21 October 1999. Recorded by Musaeva)

After the bombing of Sectors 12 and 56 people, began leaving Grozny. Planes were flying over the city almost every day, although they did not always drop bombs. The city was deserted: 70% of our neighbours had gone.

On 21 October, I, my brother, and our friend went to the Central Market to stock up on food. It took us about 4 and a half hours, driving in a Lada.

There were a lot of people at the bazaar, just like in peacetime. Aslanbek went straight off to the fish stalls. I was looking around other stalls and heard explosions. There were 4 very powerful explosions one after another. I turned towards the explosion and heard a loud whistling in my right ear. I heard that whistling for about a week afterwards. Later, when I was taking care of my brother, I sometimes fell asleep by his bed and the whistling woke me up. At the same time hundreds of shrapnel fragments were ricocheting around. I thought about my brother and ran to find him. Women were screaming and crying all around. There were wounded everywhere, severed arms and legs and blood. I saw the body of someone who had had their head blown off by the shell. The body was lying in one place and the head somewhere else. People seemed not to understand what had happened to them. Some injured people who had had limbs torn off were standing there looking strangely calm, others were unconscious.

I was not really scared. Even though in that war I was just a kid, I had already seen plenty. My brother was standing by the stalls selling household goods. He was holding his left arm, or at least what was left of it, with his right hand. He was covered in blood. His neck and face had been burned and pieces of skin were peeling off. There was an open wound on his left temple. Not a millimeter of skin on his face was a normal color; it was covered in cuts. Part of his lower lip had been torn off and he had shrapnel in both eyes. I took him in my arms, told him it was me (because he could not see anything any more) and ran to the car over pieces of slate and wood which were drenched in blood. We drove Aslanbek to Hospital No. 9. On the way, he said, „Do not torment yourself and me. Leave me; let me die." He realized he was blind. He was not groaning, but after a while said he was tired and asked me to support his injured arm and then, with his good hand free, pressed my head against his shoulder. That seemed to make him feel better.

In Hospital No. 9 the doctors did not even ask us any questions. They immediately went to work on the shattered bone, took shrapnel out of his shoulder and stitched the wounds on his face. We had already moved Aslanbek out of the operating theatre to a ward when cars and a bus full of injured people began arriving at the hospital.

What have I done to deserve this?

(The words of Makka Salamova, a victim who lived in Microregion 4, Grozny. Recorded by staff of the Filtration Camp Prisoners Association in July 2000)

My husband and I had 8 children: 7 girls, and the eighth was a long-awaited son. He was given the name of Denis, but in the family we called him Deni. From the time of the first war we had been living in Russia, where Denis was born. We only came back home in spring 1999, in May. We bought an apartment in Grozny, but before we had time to settle in properly war broke out. By this time Amin, my husband, was working at the Red Hammer Factory. He almost always took Denis with him. Already in September, though, people were leaving the city, some going to their villages and others to Ingushetia. We were among the few still living in Grozny, although there was no gas or electricity. That day, Amin took Denis to work with him as usual, and warned me they would go to the market to shop for food.

It was 21 October. Up till then life in Grozny had been uneasy, but at least there was no shelling. At about 5.00 in the evening there was a terrible explosion that shook the whole neighborhood. We had no idea what had happened. Everybody ran down into the courtyard, but there were no more explosions. About twenty minutes later, we heard a missile had exploded in Kalinin and killed several people. As time went by and my men still had not come home, I started feeling queasy. We were still in the courtyard when the first news came through about the Central Market. There were terrifying rumors that some new kind of missile had exploded over it and taken the lives of hundreds of innocent people who were completely off their guard. My legs gave way and I sat down on a bench, supported by a neighbour. I got a grip on myself and asked a male neighbour to drive me to the market, because Amin must be there as he still had not come home. He agreed immediately. We asked Raisa to look after the girls and drove there. There are no words to describe what we saw. I ran about among mutilated bodies and mangled cars, searching for my men. My neighbour tried to keep up with me, not to leave me on my own, but it was impossible. There was terrible panic all around. It was totally chaotic.

Zia, that is my neighbor's name, was the first to find our car, or at least what was left of it and my beloved men. He did not want me to come near, but I rushed to where they were with a shriek of despair and grief and pushed him aside. Can you imagine it? Both had had their arms ripped off and had multiple shrapnel wounds. Denis had lost the left side of his head, and the entire right side of Amin's body had been torn off. The shrapnel or shell must have gone straight between them. They probably never knew what had happened. Zia, may the Almighty reward him, helped me bring their remains home.

The next day we took them and buried them in our village, and after that we had no men in our house. If at least Denis had been spared... I and my husband had waited so long for him. He was to continue our family line, but evidently that was not God's will. He lived for only 2 years.

Afterwards we discovered they had used tactical surface-to-surface missiles. [President] Aslan Maskhadov told us. When they exploded, they released 6 small missiles, and those exploded up in the air, before reaching the ground. That meant they killed the maximum possible number of people who were within the missiles' operational range.

Can anyone really pretend that the soldiers who targeted that missile strike did not know they would kill the people living in the city, the women, the children and the old people included? That I will never believe. But what do they care whether I believe it or not? They have their own intentions, and obviously want to kill as many people as they can. What have I done to deserve this? How am I to feed my girls? What future do we have to look forward to?

Testimony of Hava Usmanova

(aged 28, born in Achkhoy-Martan District.
Recorded by Siddiq Bilto, ChechenPress, 20 October 2003)

She has 3 children: 2 boys aged 6 and 4, and a girl aged 18 months. This woman looks older than her years. Her expression is weary and her eyes suggest she has no tears left to cry. Several other people are present in the house. Barely able to hold back her tears, she begins her story:

„I had 3 people close to me, who cared for and protected me. My mother, her name was Maret, was killed in the early days of the war in 1999 during the missile attack on the Central Market. She sold food products there.

After burying her, my husband and I decided to move to Ingushetia. I persuaded Salman, my 16-year-old only brother, to come with us. We just managed to get settled in one of the tented camps in Ingushetia. From time to time my brother went to Achkhoy-Martan to see our great- aunt. He would stay a few days and then come back. In July 2003, Salman again went to visit her but did not return."

Going to look for him, Hava learned her brother had been detained during a security sweep and taken away by the Russian army of occupation. For several months she searched for him, but without success. She went to the military commandant's office, the prosecutor's office and other institutions and organizations of the occupying forces. Someone finally whispered that there was an FSB officer called Alihan who, in return for money, would look for people missing in this way. Needless to say, Hava and her husband had no money but decided to sell their Lada. The next day, 10 September 2003, Mahomed went off to Urus-Martan car market. When 2 days had passed and he still had not returned, Hava went looking for her husband. At the market she heard he had sold the car for $900. She looked for him practically everywhere he could possibly be.

A week later, the decapitated body of a young man was found and, from his personal belongings, identified as Mohamed. It was later learned that he had been arrested by a mobile checkpoint manned by Russian mercenaries between Urus-Martan and Achkhoy-Martan.

The woman told her story with tears streaming down her cheeks. She described some of the details at great length, needing her listeners to under- stand the depth of her pain. She concluded her tale with the words, „I do not know what the rest of my life will be like, but every time I perform namaz, I pray to God to curse this satanic Russian army and their Chechen hangers-on who are even more vile than their masters!"

She put all her pain and hatred into these words. Those present with us in the room mentioned it was time for the news. We turned on the television. They were reporting from a summit meeting of the Organisation of the Islamic Conference in Malaysia at which the Russian President Putin was speaking. He thanked the OIC for sending their observers to Chechnya to the „presidential election" and for inviting him to their summit. He went on to assure those present that Russia's Muslims were an integral and wholly respected part of Russian society. After this, the OIC delegates applauded Putin rapturously.

Hava said to me in perplexity, „You are a journalist. Give me an answer as to why an organization calling itself an Islamic conference is giving an ovation to a man who has ordered the massacre of tens of thousands of entirely innocent Muslim women, children and old people?" Hava's question forced me to think. The first excuse that came to mind was that this was politics and diplomacy.

I could not, however, find any excuse for those Muslims applauding this slaughterer of the Chechens. I told her I could not understand it myself. I did not know what to say, shocked that an Islamic platform was being provided to the bloodthirsty leader of a totally bloodthirsty state who had the murder of hundreds of thousands of Muslims on his conscience.

Now the Chechens are being openly sold out, without pretense or fine words. Praise be to the Almighty Creator, who will render what is due for every good or evil deed, be it only the size of a speck of dust! From this we

Chechens should learn one more lesson: that we must place our trust only in the Almighty Creator and in ourselves. The unity of all Chechen people is indispensable and will assuredly lead us to success, to the liberation of our land from the forces of occupation, and consolidation of the Chechen state.

The fact that some false „friends" have cast off their masks is only to the good. We will have fewer delusions about this cruel, cynical, selfish world in which nations, including Muslim nations, are ruled over by dishonest, corrupt politicians.

Tactical Missiles Used Against Chechen Citizens

(Witness statement from a victim, Raisa Hamzaeva)

On 21 October 1999, an event occurred which should have made the world shudder. A strike by tactical surface-to-surface Russian missiles was launched against unsuspecting civilians in the capital of Chechnya.

On that day of ill omen, I, Raisa Hamzaeva, was in the Central Market in Grozny at my butcher's stall. Late in the afternoon, when all the people who come to buy, or who sell or work at the market, were preparing to go home after buying food for their evening meal, there was a sudden bright flash and something exploded over the Central Market. This, we later learned, was a strike using missiles with multiple war-heads. There were similar strikes against the National Maternity Hospital on Red Frontline Fighters Street, the Central Mosque near the bazaar, and also the mosque in the suburb of Kalinin, where the men had gathered for evening prayer.

Almost 90% of the people in the market and at the mosque were killed or maimed. Newborn babies and their mothers lay lifeless in the streets and the ruins of the National Maternity Hospital, their mutilated bodies and severed heads blasted all over the place.

It is a miracle I survived, but my left arm from shoulder to wrist was mangled, I lost one eye, and shrapnel passed right through my back, tearing my stomach.

Because of the military situation, the gas, electricity and water in Grozny were turned off. The hospitals could not function, the doctors able to provide no more than first aid, give pain-killing injections and bandage minor wounds. As a result, almost all the people brought from the market, mosques and hospital died, most from loss of blood. I can be considered lucky. I survived thanks to a surgeon at the hospital who is a relative of mine. He drew blood from his own vein, which belonged to the same group as mine, and transfused it into my vein. He obtained a generator for electric light from somewhere and operated on me for 8 hours.

The operation was successful and 3 days later my relatives and I tried to drive from Grozny to Ingushetia. We were afraid we might end up under siege by the Russian troops surrounding the city, but they would not allow even the ambulance, in which I was gravely ill, through the Kavkaz border checkpoint. We were delayed there for 2 days. Every 2 hours the nurse accompanying us gave me injections of tramadol and relanium, which made me numb.

We had no choice but to turn back and returned to the hospital, which was already being bombed by Russian planes. There were a lot of injured people in the basement. The medicines and dressings ran out and then there was nothing to treat people with. It was decided to relocate the hospital, complete with all the medical staff and the wounded.

They tried sending me to Dagestan in a different vehicle, but for a month we were driving in circles round the perimeter of Grozny unable to leave because of the concentrated fire targeted on little Chechnya. It seemed as if every square meter of our country was being deluged with fire and lead of different calibres. Without dressings or medical treatment, my wounds began to fester and people had to keep their distance from my stinking body.

We managed finally to reach the Dagestan border, but no one wanted anything to do with me, probably because of the fetid smell. We paid a 1,000 ruble bribe at the Gerzel border post and entered Dagestan. My sister accompanied me everywhere.

I was in luck in Dagestan, because my mother is from Khasavyurt. By pulling strings, a hospital place was found for me, even though it was strictly prohibited for Chechens to cross the border into Dagestan. I was in hospital there for 5 months, and then another 3 with my relatives in Khasavyurt. The cost of all my treatment, medicines and other expenses was borne by my relatives.

After all that care and being confined to bed for 9 months, I finally stood up for the first time. I was very weak and dizzy but afterwards was able to walk again. I stayed a little longer in Dagestan before travelling to Baku, the capital of Azerbaijan, where I underwent 3 more operations. Even though my left arm was amputated and my left eye had been removed, I did not give up and stayed cheerful.

In hospital in Baku, I regularly heard the Russian media reporting the displeasure of the leaders of Russia that Azerbaijan was supposedly giving medical care to Chechen fighters. I, an ordinary Chechen, was outraged by the shameless statements of these barbaric Russian murderers. Where is the conscience of these savages, if they ever had one? I am a civilian, a woman, and I have had to endure so much through the evildoing of these barbarians. I have lost an arm and an eye and suffered terribly, and they have the audacity to utter these pronouncements after perpetrating such unprecedented atrocities.

Who says anyway that warriors defending their homeland should not be offered medical care? There is no internationally accepted document proposing anything of the sort! The Russians have made all this up themselves. The Chechen warriors are a thousand times better than those Russian savages who indiscriminately annihilate everybody, women, children and the old. I can testify to this genocide to anyone, any time, before any court because I not only witnessed their mass murder but was also a victim. On the day I was injured, I know for a fact, some 300 people were killed whom I knew personally at the market. And how many more died whom I did not know?

Later I learned that nearly everybody in the Grozny hospital where I was taken after being wounded ended up in Chernokozovo Prison. After the Chechen commanders gave the order to abandon the city, all the hospital staff and the wounded were surrounded as they were leaving Grozny at Alhan-Kala and seized by Russian troops. All the doctors and the wounded, bleeding and barely alive, were taken under guard to Naur District and imprisoned in the camp. For 5 months, in Chernokozovo all the wounded and almost all the medical staff, headed by the Minister of Health of the Chechen Republic, Umar Hanbiev, were beaten, tortured, savaged by dogs, and humiliated. The women who were with them, including those who were wounded, suffered the most excruciating torture and, in addition, were raped.

When I think about that, it makes me feel ill. I am horrified by the thought that I could easily have been there with them. I do not know what might have happened to me in Chernokozovo, but can only suppose I would have died, because in my condition I could not have survived prison.

But God was merciful to me and I am alive, though crippled. Life goes on.

The war and the civilian population

(From a broadcast by Andrey Babitsky on Radio Liberty, 25 March 2003)

As regards the rules of engagement in respect of military operations at the beginning of the second, and bloodiest, Chechen campaign, I have to say that the Russian side did try to set rules. I remember when part of a semi-strategic missile fell on the Central Market in Grozny, killing a huge number of people and injuring even more, Russian army officers told me a special commission was sent from Moscow to Vladikavkaz to try to establish what had happened.

I believe, though, that this colossal army grouping, which numbers some 100,000 soldiers, is highly unmanageable. So, for example, when humanitarian corridors were declared for people to leave a particular town or village which was under threat and which Russian troops were preparing to enter or bomb, the humanitarian corridor sometimes operated and sometimes did not.

Artillery and missile bombardment

(Memorial Human Rights Centre, Ryazan, Issue No. 45, 10 November 1999, http://www.hro.org/war/v16.htm)

[Since taken down from the Internet] Artillery bombardment of Grozny and Gudermes, where dozens of apartment blocks have been destroyed, is continuing. Radio Liberty's correspondent reports from Chechnya that last night surface-to-surface semi-strategic missiles with cluster munitions were fired at the Vedeno Gorge. This morning, 4 missiles were fired towards Chechnya from North Ossetia. The missile bombardment was witnessed by correspondents of Radio Liberty located in Vladikavkaz.

Correspondents report that numerous casualties have been brought to hospitals in Shali, Argun and Urus-Martan. It is impossible to treat most of them because of the absence of medical supplies, electricity and heating.

Use of special weapons by the Russian aggressors

CRI Health Minister Umar Hanbiev has analysed the results of use by the Russian aggressors of special weapons and munitions on the territory of the Chechen Republic of Ichkeria. The value of the analysis is that Hanbiev directly observed and treated people injured by these weapons while present on the territory of the CRI.

In addition to conventional weapons, the Russian armed forces used weapons of mass destruction in populated areas of Chechnya. Use of these is prohibited by the Geneva conventions.

Surface-to-surface semi-strategic missiles

These exploded in the air, showering a huge quantity of 4-sided pointed shrapnel over a very wide area and causing numerous civilian casualties among a population with neither the means nor the knowledge to protect themselves. The shrapnel causes massive damage to human tissue. Those wounded die from traumatic shock within a few minutes of being injured. This is due to the particular shape of the fragments which are „micro-bricks" 4 × 4 × 2 cm in size with sharp abrasive edges.

Such shrapnel caused major mutilation of body tissue. The sharp, abrasive edges ruptured tissue, fractured bone tissue and small fragments reaching, for example, the liver or kidney, could rupture the entire organ.

Traumatic amputation is a typical outcome when a limb is hit by such shrapnel. A chest wound caused by it looked as if „a rat had passed through the chest, devouring and scattering the tissue". Despite the vast number of traumatic craniocerebral injuries (the missile exploded in the air above the heads of people walking or standing), the proportion of victims arriving at the hospital with head wounds was only 0.6%. All the others died on the spot.

The usual ratio of wounded to killed when conventional weapons are used is 4 to 1. In the case of a missile strike the ratio is as high as 2 killed to 1 wounded.

On 21 October 1999 the surface-to-surface missile strike on the Central Market in Grozny, Maternity Hospital No. 1, the bus station and mosque produced this ratio of civilian casualties, with over 400 killed and approximately 200 injured.

Thus, the number of those killed was twice the number of injured. Further examples of equally lethal consequences of the use of this kind of weapon against civilians can be given. Later, when there were pitched battles in Grozny, the strike effectiveness of surface-to-surface missiles against the city's defenders, who were protected by shelters, was zero, despite their being used on a massive scale by the enemy. Because of this, Chechen soldiers called it „the Bazaar missile".

Indiscriminate use of force by federal troops during the armed conflict in Chechnya: missile attack on Grozny, 21 October 1999

(From a Radio Russia broadcast on 31 October 1999)

On 21 October 1999 explosions were heard in several parts of Grozny. One of these occurred at the Central Market among stalls which trade in leather clothing and food products. The following day, television reports showed destruction in the market and mangled lumps of metal, which eyewitnesses said were the remains of sur- face-to-surface missiles.

According to a correspondent of Radio Liberty, one of the explosions occurred in the courtyard of the Maternity Hospital, killing 13 pregnant women, 15 newborn babies, and 7 people waiting at a bus stop. Natalia Estemirova, a resident of Grozny, was there at the time.

Natalia Estemirova: At about 4.20 pm local time, or 5.20 pm Moscow time, I finished a television editing job. It was still light when I caught the bus. Several more people got in, so there were about 7 of us in it. I saw 3 girls and a young man crossing the road. That was the last thing I saw. I do not remember whether or not I heard an explosion after that, but I do remember a dreadful brown cloud rushing towards us from the Maternity Hospital. We dashed off the bus and towards the ruins of a nearby building. It was an old brick building and very robust. One woman and a man were running in front of me. He suddenly stumbled and fell. We ran into the ruins and then there were more explosions.

I realised only later that I must have been struck by bits of brick, and saw scratches on my arm. They must have happened at that time. We were no sooner in the ruins than a girl of about 12 was brought there with a lot of perforating wounds.

The following morning I needed to go to Nazran. I had arranged with someone I knew that his driver would take me to the bus station. The driver told me that until midnight they had been ferrying wounded people to Hospital No. 9. They had counted 75 dead bodies and 150 wounded. I asked them whether any had been in uniform. He said: „I do not think so, because they were mostly women and children."

I heard from him that the missiles had also struck in Kalinin. It is part of Grozny, and the vilest thing is that is a very peaceful part of Grozny. Kalinin is where refugees fled to during the shelling in August 1996 when the bombing was at its height. We sat it out in Kalinin for 3 days ourselves.

Actually, there was shelling there too, but not to the same extent. He told me they had brought 5 very severely injured children from there. The children had been out fetching water when they came under fire.

Presenter: According to the head of intensive care at Municipal Hospital No. 9 in Grozny, the intensive care unit alone admitted 70 casualties.

The following day, Mumadi Saidaev, director of operations of the Chechen armed forces, talked of 137 fatalities and more than 250 wounded. He said there had been explosions at the market, beside the former Post Office building, near the residence of Maskhadov, and in Kalinin in the Lenin District of Grozny. A few seconds before the explosions, bright flashes lit up the sky over the Terek Ridge north of Grozny.

Comments by officials of the Russian Federation

In the course of 22 October, officials of various ranks gave no fewer than 5 substantially different explanations of what had occurred the previous day.

Aleksandr Mikhailov, director of the Russian Information Centre, said in an interview on NTV's morning „News" programme that not a single combat mission had been flown over Grozny the previous day by federal forces and there was no use of tactical surface-to-surface missiles. Mikhailov did not rule out the possibility that the explosion in Grozny had resulted from a terrorist act prepared by the militants themselves.

The director of the FSB's Public Relations Centre, ***Aleksandr Zdanovich***, stated in an interview on Radio Russia that the FSB had no part in explosions in central Grozny and the city market, noting, however, that the FSB had „evidence that militants, believing that the crowds of people would shield them from an airstrike, had stockpiled a vast quantity of weapons, ammunition and explosives at the market. Accordingly, we do not rule out the possibility that a spontaneous explosion of ammunition may have occurred and led to loss of life."

At a press conference in Helsinki, Russian Prime Minister ***Vladimir Putin*** said, „I can confirm that there was indeed an explosion of some sort in Grozny, at a market, but I wish to draw the attention of representatives of the press to the fact that we are talking here not about a market in the usual sense of the word. We are referring to the Arms Market, as this place is known in Grozny. It is a base where arms are stored and it is one of the headquarters of criminal gangs. We do not rule out the possibility that the explosion which occurred there resulted from a clash between rival factions."

Finally the chief of the Organization and Mobilization Directorate of the General Staff of the Russian Federation, Colonel General ***Vladislav Putilin*** stated:

„There have been no strikes on Grozny at this time and the armed forces have no involvement in this incident. Due to the fact that Grozny is not presently under the control of the armed forces of Russia, there is currently no objective possibility of confirming the objectivity of the first statement issued."

In a live program „Voice of the People", in reply to questions from reporters about what had happened in Grozny on 21 October, the commander of Army Group West, Major General **Vladimir Shamanov**, stated:

Shamanov: We have a fundamental principle on which we are firmly agreed that we do not target hard-kill operations on populated areas.

Second. On the basis of objective control, individual strikes are mainly by aircraft on previously reconnoitered targets which have been confirmed by at least 3 sources. I therefore officially state that today the strikes being undertaken are directed against militant targets.

I can tell you authoritatively how this incident occurred. At the time I was relaxing. The director of electronic warfare knocked and informed me, „Comrade Commander, major signals interception in the northern sectors of Grozny." I proceeded immediately to the intercept centre where there were indications that a warlord had been killed, the war-lord's brother had been wounded, and assistance was urgently needed. In all, 40-50 network participants were operating. There was a sense of major panic. There was a sense that the strike had been so accurate that the enemy, the terrorists, were in a state of extreme confusion. This could have been caused by missile strikes by aircraft, ground forces, or precision-guided weapons.

Presenter: But here is what an eyewitness, Grozny journalist Natalia Estimirova, has to say.

Estemirova: When we talked to people it was clear that this war is being waged not against terrorists or „Wahhabis" but against a civilian population. I, for one, see this as proof that a war against terrorists is being converted into a war against a people. We have collected large amounts of corroborative evidence.

Here is what people have told us. Shamil Basaev's brother came on 6 October and demanded he be given 20 young men for his detachment. A Muslim judge and the old men refused. They said, „We do not want this; our young men do not want it." He left, and the next day they were bombed. We were told in Zamai-Yurt that fighters had come in the morning. They passed through the village at around 5.00 am, and for the rest of the day aircraft were circling overhead. People got used to them, came out, and just stared up at them. Then, completely unexpectedly, the planes struck. Young people had gathered in the centre of the village, and it was they who were attacked. These were people who had not intention of fighting.

Presenter: Thus, the highest officials of the Russian Federation and the chiefs of the General Staff have not only lied, trying to conceal the cause of the explosions in Grozny, but are also directly responsible for the massacring of the civilian population.

We are told the army is different today, no longer like the one that fought in Chechnya in 1994-6. This is what I want to discuss with Grigoriy Yavlinsky, leader of the Yabloko party.

Presenter: I want to ask you a question about what you said on television. You said our army is what it is, and at present it unquestionably requires our support. Is that right?

Yavlinsky: The meaning of my words was that our army was never trained for operations of this kind. The events of 1994-6 demonstrated that it was not ready to fight in such conditions and to resolve that kind of military problem. To make matters worse, the government to this day sees no need to pass appropriate legislative measures legalising the army's position. (Under the laws of Russia, an order by the president of the Russian Federation to use troops must be ratified by the State Duma. That has not happened. Accordingly, Mr. Yavlinsky has every reason to consider the actions of the president and the army in the Chechen Republic to be unlawful. This means that the Russian army has precisely the same legal status as the armed groups there – *Ed.*)

To this day no decision has been taken to introduce a state of emergency in Chechnya, in the Stavropol Region, in Dagestan, in Ingushetia or any- where else. It makes a very painful impression, for example, when you see Russian helicopters firing at our own riot police. Do you know how many people were killed? Thirty-five! There is a very unpleasant impression left by some of the stupid things we hear in response to the explosion at the market in Grozny. Politicians taking decisions need to understand exactly what kind of army they are sending to fight in the North Caucasus. exactly what kind of army is receiving their orders. This is an army. We are not just talking abstractions: this is something we have created. It is as it is, and it is fighting in the only way it knows how.

Of course, it is impossible to agree with everything I said. Of course, this is not a matter the soldiers and officers have to answer for. It is a matter the generals who conducted the 1994-6 campaign in a criminal manner have to answer for. I fear their knowledge and skills are little better today. Nevertheless, this is our army, the only army we have at present, and nobody else is going to defend us against gangsters and aggressors.

Understanding all this, we have to say, „Yes, we stand by our soldiers and officers who are giving their lives for the freedom and independence of our Motherland. But we have to ask the politicians whether, when they adopt their decisions, they are really taking into account what kind of army is advancing on Grozny, what kind of army is heading towards a major war in Chechnya. That today is the crucial question.

Presenter: Have I understood that correctly? When you talk about giving unconditional support to the army, you are saying that you cannot support the politicians who are sending in an army that engages in carpet bombing or bombs the market in Grozny, causing civilian casualties?

Yavlinsky: Yes, I can say I support the soldiers and officers of Russia, and always will. I absolve them personally of all blame. I am talking today about something quite different. When the prime minister gives instructions to such an army to mount an assault on Grozny, to cross the River Terek and move into the south of Chechnya, then it is he who bears responsibility for what happens there, not the army.

Presenter: Can we even consider it possible for our troops to conduct the kind of operation currently going on in Chechnya?

Yavlinsky: The problem is that large paramilitary criminal detachments have formed in Chechnya and we have nothing to oppose them with. We have nothing other than the kind of army we have. All this adds up to a very difficult situation for Russia. Unfortunately, apart from you, no one has yet asked this question. Our country is today in a very parlous situation. There are serious paramilitary criminal gangs that really threaten our freedom, life and security, and all we can counter them with is the only army we have. As a Russian politician, I will give my support to our army, our soldiers and officers.

What I have to say to the politicians in Moscow who take the relevant decisions is quite another matter. As for as an alternative way out is concerned (as I have said before and repeat now), there can be no military solution there: the only possible solution is political. It has 2 main aspects. Putin must talk to Maskhadov and Putin must seek the under- standing of the local population. Some steps are already being taken in this direction. When people tell me Maskhadov has no control over any- thing, I say, quite right: he has no control over the bandits, but he was elected by the Chechen people. If you want to find a common language with the population (and without that you have no prospect of beating the bandits), you simply must talk to Maskhadov.

Presenter: That was the viewpoint of Grigoriy Yavlinsky. That concludes our program. All the best.

PS In the conflict that broke out between Georgia and Russia in early August 2008, the Russian army, having received the go-ahead from the Kremlin, again used tactical weapons of mass destruction banned by international conventions, the surface-to-surface Tochka-U (SS-21 Scarab A). This fearsome weapon failed, however, to have the desired effect due to the fact that the Russian troops missed Georgia with their missile strike, which hit adjacent territory. They had been unable to carry out the necessary preliminary reconnaissance of the area. In other words, unlike the missile attack in Chechnya, this was an untargeted missile launch intended to sow panic among the Georgian population. A detailed report on the use of tactical missiles in Georgia can be found on the website of *Novaya Gazeta* at:

http://www.novayagazeta.ru/data/2008/67/01.html

Events in Chechnya

(Press release from Memorial Human Rights Centre, Citizens' Assistance Committee, Amnesty International)

On 16 November 1999 a press conference was held with presentations by representatives of the Memorial Human Rights Centre, Citizens' Assistance Committee, and Amnesty International who had just returned from Ingushetia.

Representatives of the Memorial Human Rights Centre and the Citizens' Assistance Committee visited the Republic of Ingushetia 6-14 November. Their work was conducted jointly with a representative of Amnesty International. They investigated the living conditions of displaced persons from Chechnya. The displaced persons were interviewed in their accommodation, hospitals, at checkpoints when entering Ingushetia, the railway station, etc.

We can state that, for civilians living in this region of Russia, the fight against terrorism, proclaimed by the leaders of the Russian Federation as the main purpose of the military operation in Chechnya, has proved a source of suffering, death, loss of health, permanent disablement, and destruction of their homes. The number of displaced persons now in Ingushetia is comparable with the total number of permanent residents of the republic.

1. On the basis of the testimony of displaced persons, independently collected in different places and at different times, we can say state that in the second half of October - beginning of November 1999 federal troops continued to mount indiscriminate air, missile and artillery strikes on populated areas in Chechnya leading to the death and wounding of civilians.

Here are just a few examples: The best known missile strike was on 21 October at the Central Market of Grozny, as a result of which more than 140 people were killed and more than 200 injured. The vast majority of the dead and wounded were civilians, including women and children.

Zulehan Asuhanov, 14, lost her right arm in the 21 October missile attack on Grozny;

A missile strike on the village of Novyi Sharoy on the night of 22-23 October: more than 16 villagers were killed and injured, including children aged between 8 and 14 years. One injured boy, Sultan Djovbatyrov, aged 9, is in Sunzha Hospital No. 1, Ingushetia.

A bomb, missile and artillery attack on the village of Novyi Sharoy on 27 October killed and injured villagers, including children. One injured child, Yusuf Yunusovich Mahomadov, 14, both of whose legs were amputated, is in Sunzha Hospital No. 1, Ingushetia.

Missile, bombing and artillery attacks on the village of Samashki on 23, 25, overnight on 26-27, and throughout 27 October resulted in many civilian deaths and injuries in the village. The worst consequences were caused by the bombardment on 27 October. For example, on 27 October an exploding shell killed Zara Mutieva and Emina (aged 12), the cousin and niece respectively of Hamsat Askhadovna Amaeva in front of her eyes. A shell which hit the home of the Mutiev family at 19 Lenin Street killed Alina Debrisheva, 12, and Zara Mahomedovna Borzoyeva, 47 years. It seriously injured Esila Abutalipovna Debrisheva, 35, who is now in hospital in Ingushetia. Also injured were Zelimhan Ikun, 14, whose right leg has been amputated and who is in Sunzha District Hospital No. 2 in Ingushetia; and Madina Avtorhanova, 22, who is in Sunzha District Hospital No. 1 in Ingushetia with a shrapnel wound in her right thigh and fractures of both forearms.

A missile strike was launched on 27 October in the vicinity of the Luch store on Lenin Street in Grozny. The media reported that on this date federal forces launched a missile strike on Shamil Basaev's house. Basaev does indeed have 2 houses in this area and, as a result of the attack which took place between 11 and 12 in the morning, those houses were partially destroyed. However, the same missile strike and subsequent bombing destroyed the adjacent blocks, no fewer than five 2-storey 12-apartment buildings, one 5-storey building and numerous single-storey private houses. There were numerous killed and injured among the residents of these houses. In addition, several taxis were destroyed and their drivers and passengers killed at a nearby taxi rank.

On 8 November, as a result of a missile hitting an apartment block on Rabochaya Street in the village of Gikalo, 10 people were killed and 12 injured. The following residents of Gikalo died: Said Arsanukaev, born 1977; Ruslan Suleymanov, born 1977; Roza Isaevna Wahaeva, pensioner. The following refugees from Naur District died: Nurdi Ibrahimovich Hanpashev, born 1953; Husein Wahovich Wisengiriev, born 1973; Waha Israpilov, born 1976; Raisa Suleymanovna Wagapova and 3 of her children.

The testimony of displaced persons suggests that air strikes are targeted at any group of cars and people in villages. In particular, there have been instances of air strikes targeting funeral processions. Thus, on 29 October a funeral procession was fired on in the village of Starye Atagi, where Tamara Chinaeva was being buried, having been killed on 27 October in Grozny in the vicinity of the Luch store. Three people were killed.

On 30 October in the mountain village of Itum-Kale the funeral was held of people killed during the bombardment of columns of refugees on the Rostov-Baku Highway on 29 October. As the procession was returning from the cemetery it was bombed. Salid Mahomed Saluyev, born 1930, and his son (in a serious condition) are in Sunzha District Hospital No. 2. Five other people were injured.

Taus Shaipov, 50, and his 8-year-old daughter Asya were wounded during a missile bombardment of the village of Gehi on 18 October.

Information has been received about many similar incidents of indiscriminate shelling and bombing of populated areas.

2. People living in Chechnya are fleeing for their lives and to save the lives of their loved ones from bombing and shelling

Incidentally, there are effectively no „humanitarian corridors" for the safe departure of civilians. There are only open „gateways" out of areas under bombardment, but no safe approaches to them. The roads are exposed to shelling and bombing. The most notorious incident was the shelling of a refugee convoy on 29 October on the Rostov-Baku Highway. The same highway has been repeatedly subjected to shelling and bombing, though less intense, on other days as well, for example, on 25 October, 4 and 6 November. These attacks also led to loss of life. Other roads are fired on. In particular, the road from Starye Atagi to the mountainous Shatoy District is under constant attack, with the result that the residents have no opportunity of leaving the area being bombed.

3. Leaving the conflict zone is more difficult than 1 month ago.

From 22 October to 1 November, the administrative border between Chechnya and Ingushetia was simply sealed. Displaced persons were then allowed to leave Chechnya, but only pedestrians are allowed out fairly speedily and without obstruction. Vehicles are held up at the Kavkaz-1 checkpoint for, at best, several days. The criteria for deciding who is allowed through and who is detained at this federal Russian checkpoint are not known. Thus, for example, 16 career criminals on the federal wanted list were allowed through, but subsequently detained by the Ingush police.

People passing through the checkpoint complain of extortion by military personnel.

At the Kavkaz-1 checkpoint the flow of people leaving Chechnya is „filtered", resulting in some being arrested and sent to a filtration point at Mozdok. Almost nothing is known about the situation there. International organisations must demand transparency about the conditions in which detainees are held.

4. According to information from the Migration Service of the Republic of Ingushetia, as of 13 November:

192,800 people (45,304 families) were registered in the Republic of Ingushetia as having come from Chechnya;

38 people (11 families) moved out of Ingushetia to temporary accommodation centres;

13,807 people travelled by rail to relatives and friends in other regions of Russia:

7,764 persons moved to northern parts of Chechnya; 1,846 persons moved to Georgia. Since 1 November: 36,175 persons have entered

Ingushetia; 7,893 people left Ingushetia for Chechnya; There are 22,000 places in settlements for displaced persons; This includes approximately 10,000 persons living in railway carriages.

The Ingush Ministry of Emergency Situations has a reserve of tented accommodation for a further 8,000 persons. However, according to even the most conservative estimates, 1,500 displaced persons per day are moving from Chechnya to Ingushetia. The considerable efforts made by the Ingush authorities to provide for refugees from Chechnya are sufficient only to avoid a sharp and uncontrollable deterioration of the situation. There is a shortage of tents and carriages, and those available are not properly heated. Many railway carriages are already overfull. In some compartments designed for 6 people, 12 or more people are accommodated. Many tents with 10 places are home to 15 people or more. We saw tents in which 10 sleeping places were home to 30 people, and to make matters worse the ration of food is calculated on the number of official places in a carriage or tent. There is a shortage of drinking water in the settlements. Although there are not yet any signs of starvation, the food supply is inadequate and there is often nowhere to cook it.

In railway carriages in the vicinity of Karabulak, where displaced people have been located since the end of October, the central supply of hot food has functioned only twice because of a lack of gas and water.

The sanitary situation in the settlements is becoming very difficult. Despite assurances from the Ministry of Emergency Situations that bath-houses are in operation, in reality people have been unable to wash there even once since the date of their arrival. According to Muhamed Aslambekovich Arsanukaev of the Russian Ministry of Health, there are many cases of head lice in the settlements, increasing numbers of people with scabies, and most of the people living in the settlements have acute respiratory infections. We have seen children covered in lice.

The number of dysentery cases is increasing. A particular threat is the approach of winter. There is insufficient wood and coal for heating the tents and carriages. In a number of carriages the heating does not work or is impaired. There is not enough water, needed for operation of the heating system in carriages. Three days of cold weather that hit Ingushetia in mid-November pushed many displaced persons to the brink of survival.

It is obvious that the military operation in Chechnya is an armed non-international conflict. The leaders of the Russian Federation who, in denial of what is obvious, describe the armed conflict in Chechnya as an „anti-terrorist operation" (last time it was „destroying criminal gangs"), are attempting to keep what is happening outside the context of humanitarian law and thus away from international control. Despite this, the OSCE Assistance Group still has a mandate to monitor the observance of human rights and humanitarian law in the conflict zone. All competent international organizations must closely scrutinise what is happening in the North Caucasus and Russia as a whole.

„Surgical strikes"

(The conflict in Chechnya in 1999. Indiscriminate use of force by federal troops during the armed conflict in Chechnya in September-October 1999)
A preliminary report Compiled by A. Cherkasov. E-mail: cherkasov@memo.ru

Introduction
1. Missile attack on Grozny on 21 October 1999
Media reports
Commentary by officials of the Russian Federation
Findings
2. Carpet bombing of Elistanzhi village on 7 October 1999
Bombing and shelling of populated areas: refugees' stories
„Friendly fire": Dagestan and Ingushetia Conclusion
This preliminary report contains information on several instances of the indiscriminate use of force by Russian federal troops in the first month of the armed conflict, up until 21 October. Memorial Human Rights Centre is continuing to collect and systematize information about violation by the parties of human rights and humanitarian law in the course of the conflict.

Introduction
Already a month has past since 22 September, when the federal air force began bombing Grozny and other major cities in Chechnya. Reporting on the progress of military operations in the North Caucasus in autumn 1999, officials of the Russian Federation, and also the media (which take their lead mainly from official statements), emphasise how what is occurring differs from the 1994-6 Chechen campaign. Relatively minor losses among the federal troops are noted, together with the greater selectivity of their operations, and the use of precision-guided weapons to annihilate terrorists while minimizing civilian casualties. It is evidently these considerations which ensure support of the government's actions on the part both of the population and the Russian political elite.

Yevgeny Primakov: Surgical strikes, if they really are precise, if smart weapons are used, and I am sure they should and no doubt are already being used, ensure that civilian casualties are minimised. (*Echo of Moscow* radio, Interview, 1 October 1999, 15:35)

Sergey Stepashin: ... And the main task today, which army units and the interior troops need to take on, along with destroying the militants' bases, is mostly using precision-guided weapons, artillery, aviation and special operations ... (Channel TV-6, „Observer", 10 October 1999; 19:55) Officials, including Prime Minister ***Putin***, are constantly talking about these techniques of warfare:

Vladimir Vladimirovich ... expressed his sincere admiration of the training and skill of pilots, and spoke with special warmth of the Russian

armorers who have created precision-guided weapons, which enable us now to strike directly at the bases where militants are concentrated and avoid needless civilian casualties. (ORT, News, 20 October 1999, 12:00)
How true are Putin's words? Even the politicians quoted above doubt their veracity:

Sergey Stepashin: ... let us objectively assess the combat readiness and capability of our forces, including our armed, forces, in terms of what we call precision-guided weapons and surveillance from space. Over the past 5-7 years not a bent kopek, forgive the expression, has been spent on these technical projects.

(NTV, „Hero of the Day", 5 October 1999, 19:40)
Russian military figures and officials talk a great deal about the use of precision-guided weapons in Chechnya, but we have only their word for this. Media reports from Chechnya, the testimony of refugees, and even an elementary comparison of statements by Russian Federation officials and spokespersons from the Ministry of Defence, give grounds to doubt the „pinpoint accuracy" and selective nature of the actions of federal troops.

1. Missile attack on Grozny, 21 October 1999

1.1. Media reports

At around 18.10 hrs on 21 October 1999 loud explosions were heard in certain districts of Grozny. Associated Press correspondent Maria Eysmont reported 118 people killed and more than 400 injured. One of the explosions occurred at Grozny's Central Market. „According to eye-witnesses, among the stalls where there is usually trading in leather clothing and food" (Interfax).

The same was reported by correspondents of Radio Liberty (22 October 1999, „Liberty Live"):

Andrey Babitsky: The strike on the Central Market in Grozny, the part where they sell not food but clothing, crockery, hardware and such like, caught people towards the end of the bazaar's day, when everybody is in a hurry after work to buy what they need. We all visited the market this morning. ... A whole sector of stalls, kiosks and awnings had been flattened by the explosion.

Peter Weill (Presenter): In other words, it was what used to be called an ordinary „collective farm market"?

Babitsky: Yes, an absolutely standard collective farm market where people sell produce. Where the missile landed they were selling household goods. We were in the inner courtyard of the General Headquarters building. We heard 2 explosions, after which we went down to the basement. The explosions occurred very close to us, literally 50-60 metres away, and we were saved by the fact that the missiles fell outside the building and impacted with the facade. According to the head of the intensive care unit of Grozny Municipal Hospital No. 9, their hospital admitted 65-70 injured people at around 1715-1720 hrs (taking account of the 1-hour time difference with Moscow – *Ed.*). (NTV, „Today", 22 October 1999)

Babitsky: We went to Municipal Hospital No. 9, and there came upon a monstrous spectacle: floors flooded with blood and a huge number of wounded. Before our eyes wounded, dead, and dying people were being brought in every second. Buses, minibuses, cars: the whole inner courtyard of the hospital was clogged with vehicles with severely injured people they were unable to bring into the hospital. I would say I counted 30 or so victims, and it was not always clear who was injured and who was already dead.

Hasin Raduyev: All the missiles exploded in the central part of the city, at the Central Market where the stalls operate almost round the clock. 61 people were killed. In Kalinin there were about 60 people in the mosque at the time for evening prayers. 41 were killed. One of the missiles exploded in the courtyard of the only functioning maternity hospital in Grozny. Thirteen women and 15 newborn babies were killed. Another 7 people were killed by shrapnel at the bus stop in front of the hospital. A lot of people were wounded at the Main Post Office, where there were several buses with passengers in the parking area at the time of the explosion.

Witnesses who survived described the incident at the market as follows:

Announcer: Local residents said they saw something explode in the air.

A female Grozny resident: Three shells came from there, 3 times, and it was like it exploded in the air, and then these fragments were flying everywhere. I don't know, it was like they exploded in the air.(NTV, „Today", 22 October 1999)

Natalia Estemirova, a Grozny resident, was getting on a No. 7 bus at this time near the former Post Office building. Hearing an explosion in the direction of the Maternity Hospital and seeing a brown cloud of brick dust coming towards them, the passengers rushed to hide from the bombard- ment in ruins opposite the Post Office. They barely had time to take cover before there were new explosions above them. The ruins did not collapse, but anybody not protected by upper floors suffered multiple shrapnel wounds. (Interview given by Natalia Estemirova to M. Zamyatin and A. Cherkasov, Memorial, Moscow, 25 October 1999)

Television reports the next day showed the destruction at the market and mangled lumps of metal which the Chechens said were fragments of surface-to-surface missiles, „huge fragments, a meter and a half in length, inscribed with numbers and letters in Cyrillic." (Andrey Babitsky)

According to the head of the intensive care unit of Grozny Municipal Hospital No. 9, they alone admitted „about 65-70 wounded people at around 17.15-17.20 hrs (taking account of the 1-hour time difference with Moscow – *Ed.*). (NTV „Today", 22 October 1999).

The lists of those killed are incomplete because many relatives took bodies for burial, and they will inevitably increase because about 100 of those injured are in a critical condition. The following day Mumadi Saidaev, chief of the Operations Directorate of the Chechen armed forces, gave a figure of 137 dead and more than 250 wounded (*Interfax*).

1.2. Comments by officials of the Russian Federation

In the course of 22 October, officials of various ranks gave no fewer than 5 substantially different explanations of what had occurred the previous day.

Aleksandr Mikhailov, director of the Russian Information Centre, said in an interview on NTV's morning „News" programme that not a single combat mission had been flown over Grozny the previous day by federal forces and there was no use of tactical surface-to-surface missiles. Mikhailov did not rule out the possibility that the explosion in Grozny had resulted from a terrorist act for which the militants themselves were responsible.

The director of the FSB's Public Relations Centre, *Aleksandr Zdanovich*, stated in an interview on Radio Russia that the FSB had no involvement in the explosions in central Grozny and the city market, noting, however, that the FSB „had evidence that militants, believing that the crowds of people would shield them from an airstrike, had stockpiled a vast quantity of weapons, ammunition and explosives at the market. Accordingly, we do not rule out the possibility that a spontaneous explosion of ammunition may have occurred and led to loss of life."

Aleksandr Veklich, director of the Joint Press Centre of the Federal Army Group in the North Caucasus, stated in an interview on ORT television that on Thursday a special operation against arms dealers had been conducted in the market district in Grozny. „According to intelligence reports, a market was found yesterday in the vicinity of the 'Stock Exchange' in Grozny, where arms and ammunition were being sold to terrorists. As a result of the special operation the market, together with the weapons and ammunition as well as the arms dealers, were destroyed. I particularly wish to stress that the operation was carried out without the involvement of troops and without the use of artillery or aircraft."

Responding to a question as to whether any civilians had been harmed in the course of the „special operation" Veklich said, „You know, civilians do not go at night to a market selling arms to gangsters and terrorists: they stay at home. So if there were any casualties, they were people who sell arms and ammunition and supply them to gangsters. "At a press conference in Helsinki, Russian Prime Minister *Vladimir Putin* said, „I can confirm that there was indeed an explosion of some sort in Grozny, at a market, but I wish to draw the attention of representatives of the press to the fact that we are talking here not about a market in the usual sense of the word. We are referring to the Arms Market, as this place is known in Grozny. It is a base where arms are stored and it is one of the headquarters of criminal gangs. We do not rule out the possibility that the explosion which occurred there resulted from a clash between rival factions."

He also denied any federal involvement in the incident, and actually disavowed what Veklich had said. „There is information that a special operation was conducted by the federal forces. Yes, such operations are conducted on a regular basis, and there is reason to believe that such an operation was carried out yesterday, but it has no relation to the events that took place in Grozny."

Finally, the chief of the Organization and Mobilization Directorate of the General Staff of the Russian Federation, Colonel General **Vladislav Putilin**, stated, „There have been no strikes on Grozny at this time and the armed forces have no involvement in this incident. Due to the fact that Grozny is not presently under the control of the armed forces of Russia, there is currently no objective possibility of confirming the objectivity of the first statement issued." Thus, Putilin too disavowed Veklich's statement.

These statements do not really require further comment. Putilin, Putin, Veklich, Zdanovich and Mikhailov themselves refute each other. However, the following day the „last word" from the federal side was an account that incorporated 3 of the versions. It was issued by **Valeriy Manilov**, first deputy chief of the General Staff: „If we turn to the most recent operations, including the one conducted on 21 October, it was a special operation without the involvement of troops and it was conducted in Grozny. As a result of this swift special operation, there was a clash between 2 major hostile criminal gangs which had long been at war with each other. This battle between the 2 gangs reached its culmination in the vicinity of one of the very large arms and ammunition stores. This storage facility is located, or rather now, was located near an area where arms and ammunition had been traded for a long time. This store, as operational intelligence indicates, contained huge quantities of all kinds of military supplies and weapons of different types, including missiles. So, anyway, as a result of this intense firefight, that we already reported about some time ago, it would appear that one of the volleys or tracer... anyway it landed in this arms and ammunition depot and there was a massive explosion" (NTV, „Today", 23 October 1999, 19:00).

1.3. Findings

Vladislav Putilin, commenting on what had happened in Grozny Market, remarked that if missiles had fallen there or if the market had been hit by 3 surface-to-surface missiles the damage would be entirely different (RTR Television, „News", 22 October 1999, 19.00 hrs).

And indeed, the explosion of one or several compact, powerful explosive devices at ground level is plainly not what occurred. Even the television reports invite a number of conclusions about the nature of the damage caused at the market. In the first place, all vertical structures (stands and so on) were undamaged, while such horizontal structures as awnings and coverings were demolished, cut in pieces, or punctured by shrapnel.

In the second place, close-ups show signs typical of the use of lethal projectiles in pellet bombs, which can be loaded into such cluster munitions as bombs and missile warheads, The blast effect from the explosion was minor and did not demolish the structures visible in television pictures. Finally, lumps of metal shown in the reports resemble the remnants of tactical missiles (guided or unguided) which are capable of carrying cluster submunitions (including pellet bombs).

The television footage and the testimony of the female resident of Grozny rule out Zdanovich's claim that there was a „spontaneous explosion of munitions", Veklich's assertion that there was a „special operation", and Putin's supposed „clash between rival gangs". If any of these were true, there would have been an explosion at ground level and, consequently, a very different scene of destruction.

Memorial Human Rights Centre already had information about the use in Chechnya of tactical missiles loaded with cluster bombs. In a survey, conducted on 10-11 October by Memorial HRC and Citizens' Assistance, of Chechen refugees in camps in Ingushetia, some refugees from Urus-Martan testified that, beginning on 8 October, several cluster bomb missiles had exploded in the Urus-Martan District and the village of Roshni-Chu. Since, however, they had apparently exploded far away from buildings and concentrations of people and caused no casualties, the refugees had not particularly drawn attention to the fact. The same information was reported by the media. „Precision-guided weapons are also being used. Last night 4 mid-range tactical surface-to-surface missiles were used against militants." (ORT Television, „Time", 11 October 1999, 2100 hrs.)

Thus, the most likely explanation of the explosion on 21 October in the area of Grozny Market is that tactical missiles with cluster bomb warheads were used.

The same opinion was expressed in an interview with Savik Shuster, director of the Moscow bureau of Radio Liberty, by President Ruslan Aushev of Ingushetia („Liberty Live", 23 October 1999). He dismissed as ludicrous the suggestion that an ammunition depot had blown up.

Ruslan Aushev: I have seen fires in military storage depots. Even when the largest depots in the Far East of Russia exploded there might be only 1 or 2 wounded. Here there is such a precise direct hit, so many dead and so many wounded. It is clear to me, as a military man, that this was a strike using tactical missiles.

According to General Aushev, people in Ingushetia and North Ossetia heard these missiles flying overhead. He believes that, in all probability, they were fired from 58 Army base near the village Tarskoye in North Ossetia. He expressed doubt that the decision to launch strikes on Grozny could have been taken at the level of commander of the army.

Aushev: No, it was taken right at the top. All decisions are taken at the highest level. ... This was use of surface-to-surface missiles ..., in principle, these can be carrying nuclear weapons. When the issue was discussed of what forces and means were to be used ... when the operation was planned, the go-ahead was given there. I think the president knows all about this. Who would take responsibility for using the missile troops without asking the president?

Finally, on 26 October 1999 in Yevgeny Kiselev's programme „Voice of the People" on NTV, Major-General Vladimir Shamanov, commander of the Russian Army Group West, admitted the explosions in Grozny on 21 October had been a missile attack launched by Russian troops.

Shamanov: Evidently use was made of the senior commander's resources.

Kisilev: What does that mean?

Shamanov: It can be missile strikes launched by aircraft or ground troops, or precision-guided weapons.

On the question of who had the right to order the use of such weapons, the answer was:

Shamanov: That is not a question for me to answer, it is a question for my superiors.

Kisilev: Do you have authority to give such an order?

Shamanov: No, I do not have such resources at my command. This makes it clear that the most senior office-bearers of Russia and the highest officers of the General Staff have not only been lying in order to try to conceal the cause of the explosions in Grozny, but also bear direct personal responsibility for the mass murder of civilians.

* * *

Missiles with cluster bomb warheads filled with submunitions with lethal projectiles are designed to destroy unprotected populations over large areas, and indiscriminate use of them, especially against civilian targets, is an unambiguous violation of humanitarian law. Russian officials, in talking about the explosion in Grozny, irrespective of whether they acknowledge or deny participation in the incident of the federal side, have 1 thing in common: they all describe the Central Market of Grozny as an „arms" market or depot, as a „headquarters of the militants", and more of the same. This is an attempt to present a civilian site as a military target and thereby to justify what was possibly a premeditated attack on civilians.

We do not yet have a list of the dead and injured and cannot assess the ratio of men to women among them. In the television footage showing the bodies of those killed, we saw only women. This market has been operating non-stop in the centre of Grozny in recent years. It has been visited by almost every journalist working in Chechnya. (Three hours before the tragedy it was visited by Petra Procházková of the Czech Epicentrum Agency.) These journalists can confirm that it has never been, and has certainly never been called, an „arms market", although anyone so wishing could buy weapons in 1 corner of it, known as the „Stock Exchange".

„...I do not know who gave that name to a section of the market where people play billiards, grill kebabs, and sell guns. We went to the 'Stock Exchange'. It is open for business. A Kalashnikov rifle costs $350, a Makarov pistol is $250, a Mukha single-use grenade launcher is $400, a rocket-propelled grenade is $1,000. ... The prices vary with the current situation in the republic. During the events in Dagestan they rose sharply, then fell. Now they have gone up again." (A. Yevtushenko, „The 'Black Market' in Grozny", *Komsomolskaya Pravda*, 23 October 1999.)

Quite clearly, what is being talked about is retail trade, not „arms depots". But even if somewhere in the market weapons were being sold, the use of armaments against the market as a whole was indiscriminate, which is prohibited under international humanitarian law. Russian officials preferred to make no mention of the mosque and maternity hospital where there was also loss of life. These are unquestionably civilian sites, and attacking them is categorically prohibited.

We should note also that the rocket attack could not have been targeting command centres, administrative offices or other capital structures because these cannot be destroyed by shrapnel from submunitions, and in fact provide good protection from them. To destroy these would require single-piece blast munitions from which, as Vladimir Putilin rightly pointed out, „the damage would have been entirely different." The strike was unambiguously against an „unprotected population".

2. Carpet bombing of Elistanzhi Village, 7 October 1999

On 9–13 October, L. Gendel, M. Zamyatin and A. Cherkasov, representing Memorial and Citizens' Assistance, interviewed refugees from Chechnya in camps in Ingushetia. In 5 testimonies, noted down in 4 different camps, refugees (including Irana Gunaeva, Daud Mahomadov, and Zaindi Imurzaev) talked about bombing of the village of Elistanzhi on 7 October, which resulted in the deaths of over 30 villagers.

Daud Mahomadov went to Elistanzhi for the funeral of his niece, Imani Muzaeva, killed in the bombing at the age of 18 in the sixth month of pregnancy. He testified that 3 streets were destroyed adjacent to the village school.

* * *

A. N. Mironov, a representative of Memorial, was in Chechnya 9-12 October 1999. Visiting the hill village of Elistanzhi, Mironov recorded an area of total devastation of 300 × 800 metres. According to the villagers, the destruction occurred at about 12 noon on 7 October as the result of high-altitude bombing.

A feature of the destruction was the overlapping of areas devastated by particular munitions, meaning that this was carpet bombing. Of those who died, 34 are buried in Elistanzhi cemetery. The majority of those on a list compiled from the testimony of the villagers are women and children. In addition, the bodies of refugees from other villages who had sought shelter in Elistanzhi were taken away by relatives for burial in their ancestral cemeteries. How many of these there were is not known. The relatively small number of fatalities is due to the dispersed nature of the buildings in the village, where houses are separated by extensive orchards and vegetable gardens.

A representative of Memorial talked in hospitals in Shali and Grozny to about 20 people wounded in Elistanzhi. Of these, only 1 was an adult male. The rest were women and children. Our observer found nothing in Elistanzhi or its surroundings that could be regarded as a military target.

* * *

The incomplete information given below about fatalities in Elistanzhi is taken from 2 separate lists. The first was obtained on 11 October 1999 in Nazran from Adlan Betmirzaev (Human Rights Committee of the Chechen Republic of Ichkeria); the second is on the website of the CRI Foreign Ministry (http://mfachri.8m.com/ru/main.htm). Where this list provides additional or different information, that is indicated in square brackets.

1. Appazov, Ramzan, retired, veteran of the Second World War, holder of many medals, (75 years old);
Artsuev, Artur, 16 (17);
Artsuev, Rahman, 12 (7);
Artsuev, Shamsuda [Shamsuddi], 11;
Artsuev, Zaur, 7 (9);
Artsueva, Taisa, 13 (10);
Artsueva, Shamsan [Shamsa], 13 (15);
Chumakov, Islam, 15 (10);
Dudaev, Aslan, 16 (26);
Dudaev, Rahman 12 (14);
Dudaev, Supian, 50 (51);
Dudaev, Usman, 44 (42);
Durdieva, Zina, housewife, 43;
Gabaeva, Madina, housewife, 43;
Gehaev, Adam, retired, 62;
Gehaeva, Aishat, pensioner, 60;
Gehaeva, Epsi, pensioner, 79;
Gehaeva, Hizhan, pensioner, 71;
Hamzatov, Adam, 4;
Ismailova, Toara (Toar), pensioner, (71);
Muhmadov, Islam, 18 (25);
Muhmadova, Malkan, 22 (25), student;
Nadaev, Sar-Ali, 18 (25);
Osupova, Imani, 21 (20);
Petirova, Satsita, 14;
Saitov, Islam, 4;

(Sapatova) Saitova, Eset, housewife, (38).

Both sources give the same death toll, but sometimes give different information about names, surnames or ages. Also, the sequence of names varies. We can deduce that the lists have different origins, con- firm each other and are reliable, but not complete. 6 people are over 60 years of age; 7 children are under the age of 14; 11 are women. Only 8 of the dead, taking the age in even just 1 of the sources, could be conditionally described as „men of combatant age", i. e., between 14 and 60 years.

According to the list of the wounded admitted on 7 October to the surgical department of Shali Central District Hospital, of 35 people, 11 were children under the age of 15, and 3 were over 60 years of age. Among the adults, aged 15 to 60 years, 11 of the wounded were women and 8 were men. According to Natalia Estemirova, who provided a list, by 21 October the total of those killed outright or who died from their injuries was 48.

Given the distribution by sex and age of those killed and injured, we can also state that the bombing of Elistanzhi was indiscriminate.

3. The bombing and shelling of populated areas: the accounts of refugees

In Ingushetia on 9-13 October, representatives of Memorial and Citizens' Assistance, L. Gendel, M. Zamyatin and A. Cherkasov, interviewed several dozen refugees in camps at Sunzha, Ordjonikidzevskaya, Karabulak, Kantyshevo, and Aki-Yurt. They were from different parts of Chechnya:

from villages in the northern Naur, Shelkovsky and Nadterechnyi Districts where federal forces were operating;

from populated areas of lowland Chechnya, which since 22 September have been bombed and fired on by federal aircraft;

from villages bordering Dagestan in the Vedeno and Nozhai-Yurt Districts that federal aircraft and artillery began bombing and shelling from the time of the operation to repulse the invasion of Dagestan by Basaev's detachments.

Interviews with the refugees showed that prior to 10 October bombing and shelling had targeted Grozny and its suburbs, Urus-Martan, Gudermes, Argun, Samashki, Serzhen-Yurt, Zandak, Vedeno, Nozhai-Yurt, Benoy, Zamai-Yurt, Pravoberezhnoye, Ken-Yurt, Naur, Naurskaya, and Goragorsk.

All the refugees said they had fled to Ingushetia to save their own lives and the lives of their loved ones from the bombing and bombardment. Almost all of them had abandoned their homes after people in their towns or villages had been killed in bombing or shelling. We have collected dozens of testimonies, but here we present just 3 examples. Each has been confirmed by accounts from refugees in different camps.

On 27 September, four Su-25 attack bombers mounted missile strikes on a residential quarter in the Grozny suburb of Staraya Sunzha. Two residential buildings were destroyed and 4 severely damaged. In the basement of a garage at 6, Batukaev Street at least 6 people were killed: from the Temirsultanov family, Ramzan, 34; his mother, Taus, 62; his 5-year-old daughter; and their friend Liza Hadjihanova (Alieva), 21, who was pregnant, together with her 2 children aged 3 years and 18 months. In the house next door Abdul Umhaev, 48, was killed.

Up to 50 people suffered injuries of varying degrees of severity. We were told about this by 5 refugees.

In Grozny in late September – early October, Russian aircraft tried for several days to destroy the television tower. As a result of numerous bombs falling in the region of Sector 56, 18 people were killed. Those injured included at least 10 children under the age of 8. We were told about this by 6 refugees.

According to refugees from Urus-Martan, Wahhabis were based in buildings of the veterinary clinic, the veterinary laboratory, and the military commissariat. Not one of these sites was damaged during bombings and missile attacks on 2-3 October. What was destroyed was School No. 7, situated across the street from one of them, killing Said-Hasan Zakriev, a teacher who was in the school. A few hundred metres from there a bomb fell into a basement where people had taken cover, killing at least 6 members of the Kerimov family: Hasan, 46; his wife, Mariam, 26; their son, Zurab, 2; Adlan, 39; his wife, Birlant, 36; and their daughter, Rita, 13. In the same basement, refugees from Vedeno were also killed: Lechi Algireyev, 43 and Kazbek Dunaev, 37. Also killed in the basement of their apartment blocks were Aset Djanaraliev, 36 and Abuyazid Rasuyev, 49. Mariam Gaitaeva, 42, was killed in the street by a burst of machine-gun fire. In School No. 1 Luiza Kataeva, 26, a teacher, was killed. Sultan Bapaev, 52, and Ahmed Hamzatov, 47, watchmen at the grain growing farm, were killed when the grain elevator was bombed. This was described in the accounts of 9 refugees.

According to the refugees, the hospitals, overwhelmed by the numbers of injured, are unable to function properly. For example, Grozny Municipal Hospital No. 9 has no electricity supply: current has to come from a generator. There is no gas supply and hence no heating. There is an acute shortage of medicines. The same is true of all the other hospitals. Indeed, the hospital in Zavodskoy District is completely closed.

4. „Friendly fire": Dagestan and Ingushetia

The above assessments relate to the territory of Chechnya which, we are told, „is not presently under the control of the armed forces of Russia". There are, nevertheless, numerous facts currently providing the „objective possibility of confirming objectivity" which are entirely real and which, indeed, the Military Prosecutor's Office is currently actively investigating. These are instances of the bombing or shelling by federal aircraft and artillery of their own units and detachments.

Already in the course of the fighting in Dagestan, Russia's air force demonstrated its inability to deliver not only „pinpoint" strikes, but even to hit the right targets. Several cases have been documented of erroneous, but targeted, bombing of their own federal units and detachments. The Military Prosecutor's Office of the North Caucasus Military District has initiated 3 criminal investigations on the basis of these facts under Article 109, „Causing Death Through Recklessness". As Deputy Military Prosecutor Igor Afanasiev reported in an interview on NTV's „Today" programme on 23 October 1999 at 1900 hrs (presenter, Mikhail Osokin; reporter, Vadim Tekmenev), these cases concern the bombing of Dagestani policemen in Botlikh, of Kemerovo riot police in the village of Karamahi, and of the 15th Armavir Special Operations Squad of the Russian Interior Ministry in Novolaksky District, with the death of 34 men.

Reporter: On 9 September 15 Squad was given just one mission: to capture Height 715.3 in Novolakskoye District, better known as the Telecommunications Tower, and hold it until reinforcements arrived. A few hours before the start of the operation, while the troops were forming up, combat helicopters struck the first blow against their own side.

Grigoriy Terentiev, first deputy chief of staff of the North Caucasus District of Interior Troops of the Russian Interior Ministry [in command of the district at that time]: At 19.45 hrs, four Mi-24 combat helicopters, oh, and with a fifth Mi-8 helicopter, hovering over us as a spotter, made 3 attacks with unguided missiles on troops preparing the assault. On the fourth attack they sprayed us with cannon fire. After the second attack, 8 men in the battle group had been hit.

Reporter: Soon the group was encircled by militants, and at just this moment the position of the Russian special forces was attacked 2 times more from the air, this time by Su-25 attack bombers.

Pavel Urlanov, commander of 2 Group, Armavir Special Operations Squad: about 6 attack runs were made, 3 of them against us.

Reporter: Nothing helped the commandos: not flares, not the gigantic logos on their hardware, which can easily be seen even from 200 metres up.

Igor Afanasiev: If there were instances of negligence, for example by one group or another, the aircraft, or those directing them to the target, what the combat missions were and where, whether ground troops were supposed to be there ... We are in the process of checking all that. We will establish the facts objectively. When we have established all the facts, I imagine the guilty will be punished.

The above are not by any means the only cases of friendly fire attacks by federal aircraft on their own units. The prosecutor omitted to mention the bombing of the Mahachkala riot police in Karamahi.

Overall, according to Colonel General Mikhail Labunts, commander of the North Caucasus Military District of the Russian Interior Ministry, who was in charge of federal troops in the vicinity of Karamahi, up to 40% of federal losses there were caused by Russia's own air forces. They were able to take the village only after aircraft ceased to be used. The same sort of thing went on in Ingushetia. According to information of the Interior Ministry of Ingushetia, on 7 October a pair of helicopters systematically shot at the East-44 Ingush police checkpoint until the commander of a federal unit situated on an adjacent height told them they were firing at their own people. All the buildings and 3 vehicles were destroyed. Additionally, as of 10 October, 7 instances of shells landing in the vicinity of populated areas were registered which appeared to be random or erroneous. At the present time, these incidents are also under investigation by the Military Prosecutor's Office of the North Caucasus Military District.

Conclusion

All this is indicative of unsatisfactory performance on the part of pilots, intelligence agents, and management. Even on territory controlled by Russian Federal forces, units were often fired on whose location should have been reliably known. The obvious conclusion is that there are no grounds to claim military operations in Chechnya are being conducted exclusively with precision targeting of firepower. The territory „is not presently under the control of the armed forces of Russia, there is currently no objective possibility of confirming the objectivity" of any statement issued. There is absolutely no reason to believe that it is now possible to strike directly at the bases where militants are concentrated and avoid needless civilian casualties."

The above allows us to state that air operations there are equally „pinpoint accurate", i. e., indiscriminate. As a result, blunders were inevitable both in respect of the bombing of „legitimate" targets and of attacks on civilian targets.

26 October 1999

Shelling and bombing of Chechnya

(September-November 1999)

Having repulsed the attacks by militants on Dagestan, the armed forces of the Russian Federation began gradually, from the end of September 1999, to move military operations into Chechnya. Air raids and artillery shelling led to mass migration of the population of the Chechen Republic. Columns of cars with people and their household goods made for areas which seemed safe: some sought to leave Chechnya altogether, while others headed for the northern Nadterechnyi District. Others made for the foothill and mountain towns and villages. Fighting on the outskirts of Grozny and in several other parts of the republic and the bombing of the mountain villages caused a new wave of people desperately seeking safety.

Starye Atagi was one of the places where streams of refugees intersected and some of them settled there. Information collected by the village administration suggests that in winter 1999/2000, the population of Starye Atagi was around 22,000.

In turn, some natives of Starye Atagi began leaving their village, and they were to be among the first casualties. On 5 October 1999, the Mezhidov family of 5 were killed by tank fire near Znamenskoye in Nadterechnyi District. Oleg Semenovich Mezhidov, who received his name and patronymic in an orphanage; his wife, Movlat Lvovna; their children Beslan, born 1969; Amin, born 1973; and 14-year-old Sveta were buried by local people. In the same area a helicopter attack on a car on 10 October left 60-year old Isa Usamovich Nahaev and 2 other men with him dead.

In October and November, Russian aircraft subjected the entire territory of the Chechen Republic to missile strikes. According to official Russian statements, these were exclusively „surgical strikes" for the purpose of destroying an armed enemy with minimal civilian casualties. Numerous reports from the areas bombed, however, undermine these claims.

Just as during the first Chechen war, Russian troops again used weapons which were manifestly not designed for selective, genuinely precision strikes. The missile attack on the centre of Grozny on 21 October received widespread publicity beyond the borders of Chechnya.

Tactical Tochka-U (SS-21 Scarab) missiles with cluster bomb warheads equipped with pellet bombs were used. One missile exploded over the Central Market, where there were the most victims. Two others exploded at the Maternity Hospital and Main Post Office building. As a result, approximately 140 people were killed and over 200 injured. The vast majority of the casualties were civilians, including women and children.

Among the victims were villagers from Starye Atagi: Liza Ezerhanova and 20-year-old Shamil Elbuzdukaev died on the spot and Aina Mudarova, seriously wounded, died in hospital 2 weeks later. Uwais Elbuzdukaev (born 1953) had his arm blown off and sustained multiple shrapnel wounds to his chest, head, and arms. Wounded beside him were his young daughter and female cousin who sold haberdashery at the market.

Air strikes were targeted at any gatherings of people. Thus, in Starye Atagi on 28 October during the funeral of 60-year old villager Tamara Chankaeva, killed along with her 12-year-old granddaughter during the bombing in Grozny, 2 aircraft fired on the funeral procession at the cemetery. As a result, 1 person was killed and 5 were wounded, a bus was burned out and 6 cars damaged.

On 29 October, Starye Atagi received its first mention in official bulletins of the press service of the Russian Ministry of Defence. According to the report, „the villagers of Starye Atagi held a rally demanding the expulsion of armed gangs." The report was a complete fabrication and is an example of the work of Russian military propagandists conducting an information war. At this time there were no armed groups in the village and, accordingly, no demonstrations against them by local people.

Bombing and missile strikes forced part of the civilian population to seek refuge in neighboring countries. However, already on 29 September the interior ministries and directorates of a number of territories and republics that were part of the Russian Federation received tele- phoned orders to close their administrative borders to people attempting to leave the Chechen Republic.

The only person to refuse to obey this instruction was President Ruslan Aushev of the Republic of Ingushetia, with the result that there was a great influx of refugees into Ingushetia fleeing the fighting in Chechnya. On 22 October, however, Russian troops sealed the border between Ingushetia and Chechnya, preventing further civilians from crossing. On 26 October, Russian state media broadcast an announcement that a „humanitarian corridor" would be opened through the monitored Kavkaz-1 checkpoint to allow people to leave Chechnya for Ingushetia.

This post was on the Rostov–Baku Highway at the border between Chechnya and Ingushetia.

Hearing that a corridor was to be provided, thousands of people decided to take advantage of the arrangement, but on 29 October travel to Ingushetia was not in fact permitted.

Hundreds of vehicles with refugees which had accumulated at the checkpoint began to reverse and return along the Rostov-Baku Highway towards Grozny. Near the village of Shaami-Yurt, however, the column was suddenly attacked by aircraft that fired several missiles at it. Among the dozens of dead and wounded were again villagers from Starye Atagi: Dashala Yusupova, 65, had an arm severed, and Halipat Shapieva, 60, was seriously injured. Both later died from their wounds.

Russian pilots positively went hunting for any cars, tractors, etc. driving outside the confines of towns and villages. It was relatively safe to travel on roads in Chechnya only in fog, at night, or early in the morning as the aircraft usually began flying only from 1000 hrs. Ignoring this led to trouble. On the afternoon of 30 October Husein Shahgiriev, 26, was killed on the road near Starye Atagi. He was on his way home with firewood when his truck was attacked by a dive-bomber. Facing a severe winter without gas or electricity, the villagers of Starye Atagi hurried to stock up with firewood.

The problem was that the nearest forest was 10–12 km away and could be reached only along the highway to Shatoy, which was subject to attack from the air.

In November the outskirts of Starye Atagi and the roads leading into the village were repeatedly subjected to missile strikes. This was despite that fact that there were no military targets, fortifications, bases or weapons caches in or anywhere near it. The elders were able to persuade Chechen fighters not to enter the village, in order not to endanger the lives of the thousands of local residents and refugees. Many hoped that the war would pass by Starye Atagi, and decided to wait there for the troubles to be over. People stocked up with paraffin, food supplies and other essentials, of which the price rose sharply. On 3 November, a clear, sunny day, a Russian attack aircraft launched a missile attack on the western outskirts of the village. The pilot evidently chose the site very deliberately: it was the crossroads of the Grozny-Shatoy Highway which passed through the village and a road leading into its centre. Here there was a bus stop, and also people selling petrol, meat, fruit and beverages. The missiles exploded in this very small area, killing 2 women: Yaha Djabrailova, 55, and T. Tsamaeva, 25. Another casualty, Malik Suleymanova, a refugee from Chishki, died of her injuries a short time later. Five other people were injured, including 2 children of the Dadaev family who were in a Lada car: a girl aged 6 had her skull injured and was unconscious for 9 days but miraculously survived; a 3-year-old boy suffered mild injuries and was concussed. He was prematurely discharged from the hospital owing to a large influx of injured people. The car's owner, Mehkan Hamzatovich Apaev, 45, was seriously injured, suffering forty large and small shrapnel wounds, burns, and concussion.

It should be recorded that the surgery department of the Starye Atagi District Hospital, under the direction of Andarbek Bakaev, continued to function throughout the period of the fighting, despite being understaffed and lacking medicines.

On 5 November, night-time bombing of the northern outskirts of the village partly destroyed the flour mill, brick and tile workshops, and wrecked 2 private cars. The following day, 2 people driving along the highway were seriously injured after being fired on from the air.

In the afternoon of 12 November, a missile strike damaged several houses in Pochtovaya and Shosseynaya Streets. A villager, Aset Mugaeva, and a woman refugee were injured.

On 18 November, 2 fighter aircraft staged an aerobatic „air show" above Starye Atagi. Many villagers came outside to watch the spectacle. The aircraft suddenly mounted a psychological attack, rapidly losing height and going into a dive on the village. The frightened villagers, mostly young children and women, fled in panic to hide in basements, but no strike ensued. On the southern outskirts of the village that day, however, 2 helicopters used up all their ammunition attacking the mill. On 29 November at around 12 noon, bombs were dropped on the quarry in the north of the village. Said-Mahomed Elmurzaev who was at work had a leg ripped off and died that night in the hospital. The next day a car was destroyed on the road near the village by a „surgical strike". The driver and passengers survived because they saw the planes turning back to attack and got out in time.

On 24, 25 and 30 November, Starye Atagi featured in communiques of the press service of the Russian Ministry of Defence as one of the populated areas „in the vicinity of which air attacks struck at concentrations of militants, their hardware and bases".

As Russian troops moved nearer, the main concern of the local administration and elders was to preserve the village from destruction and the population from extermination. The imam of the mosque and authoritative villagers appealed to young people not to undertake any provocative actions that might have serious consequences for the village. Meanwhile, in early November, the situation in Chechnya was considered in Strasbourg at a session of the Parliamentary Assembly of the Council of Europe. In its resolution of 4 November 1999, PACE called upon the Russian Federation not to bomb the civilian population, to cease fire and start a peaceful dialogue with the elected Chechen authorities. The Assembly also called for all those responsible for terrorist acts, human rights violations and kidnapping to be brought to justice in the courts, and all hostages immediately released. They had issued a similar call the month before.

Memorial Human Rights Centre

Bombardment of the „humanitarian corridor" on 29 October 1999 on the Moscow-Baku Highway at the border with the Republic of Ingushetia

Medna Chuchuevna Isaeva testifies

(Recorded by Libhan Bazaeva, 24 April 2000)
„I worked in a drug treatment clinic as deputy medical consultant in charge of accounts. I several times heard that a corridor for refugees would be provided on 29 October. On 28 October I and my family arrived at the checkpoint at Assinovskaya on the highway leading to Nazran in order to confirm when the corridor would be opened. Soldiers at the checkpoint replied that the corridor would be provided on 29 October, that is, the following day. Many other people waiting at the checkpoint heard this.

Believing what we had been told, all my relatives, 14 of us, left Grozny heading for Nazran. At about 0600 or 0630 we approached the Kavkaz-1 checkpoint. There was already a 1-kilometre long queue of vehicles. We went on foot to talk to the soldiers and they told us that the order should arrive at 9 o'clock to start allowing refugees through. That is what they were waiting for. The sky was overcast and it was drizzling. While there were thunderclouds, the soldiers continued to say they were waiting for the order. By 1100 the clouds broke up and the sky became clear. Then one of the soldiers came out to the crowd and said, „The corridor for refugees will not be opened today and we have no exact information about when it will be."

The cars began turning back. People were walking between them. The column began moving back, but very slowly because the cars were in several rows and could not turn round quickly.

When the sun came out, we saw planes in the sky. They calmly turned above the column and started bombing the refugees' cars. The first bomb I saw landed on a large vehicle with refugees and their belongings, a cold storage truck. I heard the next one behind. The driver stopped our minibus and we quickly started getting out. My 2 children were the first out, then my daughter-in-law. In front of my eyes, all 3 were thrown to one side by a blast at the edge of the highway. I was flung back into the minibus by a piece of shrapnel. My right forearm was wounded. When I recovered consciousness, I got out and ran to the children but they were already dead.

My daughter-in-law had been killed too, with shrapnel in her heart. Wounded people and dead bodies were lying all around. Until the planes had completely run out of bombs, they turned several times, dropping bombs on us, a column of refugees 12-14 kilometres long.

At about 1 o'clock in the afternoon we set off back home, sending the wounded on one vehicle to the hospital, and loading bodies on the other. The wounded were taken to Atagi. They did what they could for them there and sent them home. The flow of wounded people was end- less and it was too dangerous to leave them at the hospital because we were afraid it would be fired on. A week later we were taken to Nazran and recovered there.

To get death certificates for my children, I had to obtain a writ in the Nazran law court, because we needed proof they had been killed by being bombed by Russian planes. Afterwards, in Moscow, I filed a complaint with the European Court of Human Rights."

Zara Avganovna Shapieva testifies

(statement also signed by Hanifat Djamulaevna Shapieva and Avgan Mahomedovich Shapiev)

„We were living in Grozny when there was an announcement on the radio and television that a corridor for refugees would be opened on 29 October 1999. At the time, our relative and neighbour Dashalu Yusupov said we only had 6 more days to wait before the opening of the corridor, but on 27 October, our October District was bombed so heavily that we lost hope of staying alive. We just remained down in the basement of our apartment block. That day, the shock wave from a bomb threw me off my feet, and I fell into an open manhole. I injured my knee. My mother was only just able to pull me out of the hole and carry me to the basement.

We decided not to wait for them to open the promised corridor but to drive to our relatives in Starye Atagi, and then on 29 October drive in the direction of Ingushetia. So, in the evening of 28 October 5 of us (our relatives Dashalu Yusupov, born 1930; his wife, Arpat Yusupova, born 1936; my parents, Hanipat Djamulaevna Shapieva, born 1935 and Avgan Mahomedovich Shapiev, born 1926 and I, Zara Avganovna Shapieva, born 1957, hurriedly drove off to Starye Atagi in a Lada to the Bashirovs, our relatives. The Yusupovs' son, Ramzan, was driving in a second car with his wife. We arrived safely and stayed with them overnight on 28 October.

On 29 October we left at 5.00 am in 2 cars and drove along the high- way leading to Sleptsovsk in Ingushetia. We were early, just No. 187 or 188 in the queue. There were huge numbers of cars and people. The cars were parked in 3 rows. We waited until 10 o'clock, but after 10 o'clock they announced that the corridor would not be opened. The cars began turning. There was a traffic jam and the cars could turn only very slowly. A huge number of cars were moving very slowly.

At about 12 noon there was suddenly a loud bang. When I regained consciousness, I saw my mother to the left of me was covered in blood, and my father, who had been sitting in front, was not there at all. Our relative, Arpat Yusupova, was also covered in blood. Dashalu Yusupov's arm had been blown off and he was already unconscious. The only people still alive and able to move were me and Arpat Yusupova. We started pulling the wounded out of the car, my mum and Dashalu Yusupov. At that moment I saw my father lying at the side of the road. Arpat and I dragged the wounded into the drainage ditch along the side of the road. At that point, I saw a shell hit a car which was driving away and it was blown to pieces. You could hear bombs exploding. When the planes flew off, I ran out of the ditch, searching for help. I needed a car to take the wounded away but everybody was in a panic. All over the road, on the asphalt there were dead and wounded people, parts of human bodies, human flesh. Behind, a bit further away, was a smashed bus. I remember the dead bus driver. His hands were still holding the steering wheel but he was headless. People were running away from the road out into the field. There were so many women and children in that field.

I ran down the road calling for help. Just at that moment a Niva off-roader appeared from the direction of Shaami-Yurt. They stopped beside me and 2 young men jumped out and helped. They took all my wounded to Urus-Martan. There was no room in the car for me and I was left standing in the road but then, luckily, Ramzan arrived. He had just driven ahead a short distance when the bomb fell. He took me to the Urus-Martan hospital. We moved our family members from Urus-Martan to the hospital in Starye Atagi. My mother died 8 days later in the hospital, on 9 November 1999. My father died 25 January 2000. Dashalu died without regaining consciousness just 2 days later, on 2 November 1999. Arpat Yusupova had only minor injuries and she survived. I was wounded by small pieces of shrapnel. A nurse treated my wounds and I looked after the wounded until they died.

I will never forget that bloody day, those parts of human bodies lying all over the road, the terrible wailing of women from everywhere. There were so many dead bodies all around me. We buried our three.

I believe this was premeditated murder of our people. They deliberately assembled people, announcing the opening of a humanitarian corridor on television and radio so as to get us concentrated in one place, and then they cold-bloodedly killed us with aircraft, wanting to kill as many as possible.

I live now in Kantyshevo, at No. 22 Djabagiev Street, in the house of Bisolt Dzaurov who selflessly let us into the house and helps us to this day. At first we lived with Ahmed Dzaurov, who also helped us."

Testimony of Zina Abdulaevna Yusupova and Dashalu Yusupov of the refugee convoy near Shaami-Yurt on 29 October 1999

We left Grozny on 29 October in a minibus with a convoy of refugees. There were 12 of us and a 2-month-old baby. At about 8.00 am we were at the border with Ingushetia. There were no more than 10 vehicles ahead of us. The driver got out and went to ask the soldiers whether they would let us through. He was told the border would be opened at around 9 o'clock.

We stood until 10.00 and only then were we told the border was not going to be opened and we needed to go back.

It had been raining since early morning, but by 11.00 it had cleared. By then we had to recognize that we were not going to be allowed through. Everybody started turning their vehicles and leaving. There was a traffic jam, so people were driving very slowly, literally at walking pace. The column was 12 kilometres long. As we approached Shaami- Yurt we saw 2 planes. They began releasing heat-seeking missiles. I wondered out loud:

„Do you think it is us they are intending to bomb?"

Madina said, „No, probably there are some fighters somewhere. They are hardly going to bomb a refugee convoy."

In less than 5 minutes, though, a missile hit the driver in the car ahead. He was evidently killed instantly, because the car swerved round violently. We jumped out of our own vehicle (Ilona, Said-Mahomed and I). There was another explosion, and I felt as if I had been squeezed very hard.

When I began to regain consciousness, I saw the children were lying there, dead, holding hands. I stood up and stared at them in bewilderment. There were people in the ditch and they dragged me in there. Then there were another 8 such strikes. People were shouting, „Get down!", but I thought that if I lay down I would have an arm or a leg torn off. Then I jumped up again and ran back out to the road and saw Madina lying on the bodies of her children. „Come over here!" I shouted, but Madina said, „No, I want to die together with them!" There was another woman lying there. She was wounded in the chest and her leg had been blown off.

Our minibus was still in one piece. Of those who had been travelling in it, Ilona and Said-Mahomed and Madina's children had been killed. Some of us were wounded: Madina in the forearm; I had a perforating wound in my neck, a gutter wound on my arm, and a shrapnel wound in the thigh; Mahomed, Madina's nephew, had a shrapnel wound in his back; Aslanbek had perforating wounds in both legs; Mahomed's mother was concussed.

We picked up the bodies of the children of Ilona and Said-Mahomed under fire. The boy had died from a stomach wound and the girl was headless. Her left leg had been completely mutilated. We took a wounded woman called Asma too, but she died on the way back. Aslanbek was her son. Another woman died, our neighbour. A piece of shrapnel entered her heart and came out her back. There was clothing and lumps of flesh lying everywhere, in the roadway and up in the trees.

We believe the traffic jam was created deliberately."

Libhan Bazaeva testifies on 15 April 2000 in Nazran

I, Libhan Bazaeva, lived in Grozny, at 56 Kaluga Street. After the Staropromyslovskii District of Grozny was bombed and had ground-to-ground missiles fired into it, staying in the city was a death sentence and our whole family decided to leave. On radio and television, on the ORT and RTR television channels, there were announcements that humanitarian corridors would be opened on 29 October for refugees to leave. Because there was such massive bombing of the city, we left on 26 October and went to stay with relatives in Gehi until 29 October. For 2 weeks there were announcements on radio and television that a corridor for refugees would be opened on 29 October. That day, after 5 o'clock in the morning, we drove along the highway leading to Nazran. When we arrived at our destination our cars were Nos. 384 and 385 in the column. A queue of cars formed behind us which was 3-4 times longer than what was ahead. We estimated that there were far more than 1,000 vehicles in the column. It consisted of cars, trucks, and large and small buses.

People were asking the soldiers when the corridor would be opened. At first they said it would be at 9 o'clock, but then their answers became vaguer. They said they did not know themselves and their officer had driven off to find out what was happening and they were just waiting for their orders. Much later, a soldier, probably an officer, came out to a crowd of people right beside the checkpoint and stated that the corridor would not be opened today and it was not known when it would be. In a very commanding tone he said people should leave the checkpoint immediately and clear the road. People were indignant and confused and slowly began to turn their vehicles round. The traffic moved very slowly. It was difficult, because the vehicles were in 3 rows, so every now and then there were traffic jams.

The rain that had been drizzling since early morning, stopped, the sky cleared and the sun came out. It was after 11 o'clock when our cars drove past Hambi-irzi and were approaching Shaami-Yurt. We were travelling in 2 cars: a white Lada and a dark blue UAZ off-roader.

I was in the first car with my husband and his friend, and my son and 2 of my husband's nephews and the wife of one of them were in the second. Our UAZ was several cars behind us. When we came to a small bridge near Shaami-Yurt, we suddenly heard bangs and explosions.

Our car was thrown to the left side of the road. A mass of broken glass, stones and earth hit me from the back through the rear window. We jumped out. I realised that the first of 4 bombs had fallen behind our car and, as my son and his cousins were driving behind us, I rushed back to look for him. I saw that anyone still able to move had either taken cover in the roadside ditches or was running over the fields away from the highway. I was probably in shock, because I felt no fear, no horror at that moment. I just wanted to reach my son, to find his car. As I was breathlessly running up that road I saw, first, a red Lada with a man sitting in the driver's seat, killed or wounded, and a woman next to him crying for help. Next I saw a big LAZ-type bus. The back, almost a third of it, was completely severed and the bodies of dead and injured people were lying in the road. In the front part of the bus people, wounded or dead, were motionless in the seats. Next there was a dark grey vehicle that looked like an ambulance. Its top had been opened, like a tin can. Alongside these 2 vehicles, spread over the whole width of the road, were bodies, many of them ripped into pieces. I saw severed arms and legs. Further along, on the right side of the road, was a big Kamaz truck. I could not see what was in the back but blood was pouring out of the slits in the side of it. I must have run about 100 metres, and in that stretch of the road as I recall I saw 40 or 50 dead bodies.

When I reached my son's car, I saw him climbing out of the roadside ditch with an injured child in his arms. It was a little girl aged between 7 and 9. I saw she was fatally wounded. The whole of the back of her head was shattered. He put her in his car and shouted to me, „Mum, I'll take her to the hospital in Achkhoy-Martan." A young man looked out of the ditch and shouted, „There is another injured girl: take her too." My son and his cousins picked the wounded girl up and carried her to the car as well. The boy who had pointed her out also had an arm injury but he was able to stand. They put him in the car too, quickly turned and headed towards Achkhoy-Martan. It all happened very quickly. I only had time to shout to them that we were alive but our rear tyres had been punctured.

They drove off with the wounded and I ran back to our car, again seeing dead and wounded people in the road. We put an old lady in our car who was running about looking for help, and decided to drive off the road because the planes might come back at any moment. We managed somehow to drive on the hubs to Shaami-Yurt and entered the village. The villagers rushed out to help us, quickly found 2 wheels some- where and replaced our damaged ones. After that we took a country road to Gehi, from where we had set out in the morning. There had been no time to arrange anything with my son, but we hoped that when he left the Achkhoy-Martan hospital he would have the sense to come to Gehi without driving on the highway. We waited and waited, but there was no sign of him. Meanwhile, we saw planes fly back again and again over the highway to bomb almost every 10-15 minutes. We waiting for 6 hours in an agony of suspense and inwardly prepared ourselves for the worst. When it was already dark and the planes had stopped flying, after 7 o'clock in the evening, they appeared in the courtyard without a car and with their clothes in tatters. They told us what had happened.

After leaving the injured at the hospital, they went back to the highway, remembering that we had been left there with a damaged car. When they got to Hambi-irzi, they saw planes flying back over them, jumped out of the car and took cover in the ditch, and people in other cars who had come back for us jumped out too. The first bomb destroyed our car, and a second fell on the ditch on the opposite side of the road where people from other cars were trying to hide. They realised the planes would come back again and again to hunt people down, and started dashing from one pit to another towards Hambi-irzi. Like that, they made it to Hambi-irzi and hid in the basement of a building there. They waited until 6.00 pm for the bombing to stop, and after that came back to Gehi on foot. Our car had been completely wrecked by a direct hit and of course all our possessions, like clothes and bedding, had been destroyed.

That is how we miraculously survived among hundreds of other people who were killed.
The bombing of the „humanitarian corridor" for refugees started at 11.30 in the morning and went on until after 6.00 pm.z

Firing on the „humanitarian corridor" on 29 October 1999: testimony of eyewitnesses

(Aset Mazhaeva (Gehoeva), witness of the firing on a refugee convoy)
Almost 4 years have passed since that tragic day, but even now it is as fresh in my memory as if it were yesterday.

My sister and I and a friend had decided to travel to Nazran. On 27 October the bombing of Grozny started and lasted well into the evening. On 28 October they started bombing early in the morning, but by then we were already on our way, leaving the city for the village. We got to Gehi, intending on the morning of 29 October to leave for Nazran in Ingushetia. For the past 2 weeks all the Russian media had been announcing that on 29 October a „humanitarian corridor" would be pro- vided for those wishing to get out of Chechnya, where an undeclared war was already raging. A couple of weeks before that date, all the roads out of Chechnya had been sealed, and 3 or 4 days later they started announcing, „Everybody who wishes to get away from the bombing in the republic will have an opportunity to leave on 29 October in all directions." That meant, towards Stavropol in Russia, Dagestan, and Ingushetia. It was also stated that anybody who stayed in their homes would be considered criminals or criminal accomplices.

Because of that, hundreds of thousands of people collected all that was most precious to them and took to the road, in the hope of avoiding the fate likely to befall those who stayed. We were all forgetting that we are Chechens, and this meant that the entire Chechen people, young and old, were being classed as criminals. „A criminal people!" In our naivety we had not recognised that yet.

So, on the Baku-Rostov Highway by the morning of 29 October 1999 there was already a 12-kilometre long queue of cars 3-4 rows deep. I was told that by a friend of mine in April 2000, when I was already working for Memorial. It was only after 6 months I learned that on that day columns of refugees were shot on all the roads of Chechnya, because the roads were packed full of cars with people and their belongings who were trying to get out of the republic. People had brought with them all their best, most valuable possessions. Many, anticipating that there would be a queue, had slept on the highway.

On that day our brothers did not let us go anywhere. They said there would be time enough later for us to leave, and nobody could be sure yet whether they would open the roads or not. I believe that saved our lives.

I remember, as clearly as if it were today, that there was a thick fog that morning, and I was unaccountably very glad to see it, although I was feeling terribly restless. In the morning my friend's brother came and, confirming that we were not going to leave, went back to Zakan-Yurt where he was staying with their mother. The fog was beginning to lift, and for some reason I felt more and more anxious.

Then, by 11 o'clock, the fog had cleared completely and 2 planes appeared in the sky. They flew very low over the village and, beyond the village limits, dived and each launched 2 missiles at some target. Then they soared up into the sky, but that was only so they could dive again and launch their next couple of missiles. They flew away, but before long another pair of planes appeared. They flew in the direction of Shaami-Yurt and we could hear missiles and bombs exploding. As the crow flies, it is only 3-4 kilometres from Gehi to Shaami-Yurt. My friend was very worried because her brother had been driving along that road. I reassured her as best I could, telling her they would not shoot at a road and they must be shooting at something in the fields or forest. I was well aware, though, that the roads had often been fired on by planes before. Because of my work I had many times seen people who had been shot on the roads.

That day, though, I did not want to believe anything like that was possible, because I knew the road was inundated with cars and people. Our neighbour had driven to the border in the morning, found it was not going to be opened, and came back home. He said it had been very difficult to get off the highway.

Meanwhile there were more and more planes flying in. We thought they must be bombing Maskhadov's „army". At about1400-1500 hrs the bombing stopped, and half an hour after that we heard terrible news. We learned that the column of refugees had been fired on in the road near Shaami-Yurt. Of course, in our worst nightmares we could never have imagined the scale of the massacre. A huge number of people had been killed and even more had been wounded. To the present day there is no way of finding out the exact number of people killed.

I hope very much, though, that it may be possible to establish that some day.

The Road

(Zara D., The Chechen Times, July 2004, Netherlands)

A road. Cars of different makes, trucks, heavy Kamaz lorries laden with household goods. In the back, sitting on top of blankets and mattresses, are old people, women and children. On one of the trucks there is a rickety chair among all the belongings, a symbol of the absurdity of this exodus. Suddenly, there is a droning in my ears, lightning dazzles my eyes. The droning grows louder and louder. Several Sukhoy attack bombers hurtle towards us, roaring and screaming. I cringe. It is going to start! A-ah-ah! I wake in an icy sweat. I can't breathe, as if a soldier in heavy canvas boots is standing on my throat. My head is compressed by an iron hoop.

Armen and Margot are leaning over me.

„What's wrong? Why are you groaning like that?"

„I dreamed of hell," I say almost inaudibly, and start silently to weep. After a short stop we continue our journey, but all I can see is that road. I do not understand what is happening, where I actually am, why I am in this car with strangers. Who are they? I cannot shake off the feeling that I am still dreaming. I am still seeing that appalling road on 29 October 1999.

We had headed in 2 cars for Nazran at about 8.00 am. In one were Avalu's 2 sons, in the other Avalu and his wife Amnat, Tukhan and his wife Seda, and me. Avalu and Tukhan sat in front and we in the back.

Grozny was being bombed every day; it was too dangerous to stay there. After the attack on 21 October, when surface-to-surface tactical missiles were launched at the Central Market, the National Maternity Hospital and the central mosque in Kalinin, killing many civilians, people fled from Grozny in panic, even those who had been determined to stay this time to protect their houses and property. They remembered coming back after the first war to find their homes looted. The Russian soldiers stole everything, and what they could not carry (furniture, refrigerators and televisions), if you were lucky, they just shot up. More often, though, they burned or blew up houses after looting them. In the 3 years between the first and second wars, many people had built new houses in place of those destroyed, and bought new furniture and things for their homes.

„We are going to stay at home, and if there is a new war, we will defend our house. We are not going to rebuild it for a fourth time!" my friends and relatives told me. They had no idea what they would face this time.

Dagestan refused to allow Chechen refugees in. In the Priterechnyi District in the north there was fierce fighting. On 27-28 October, Grozny was intensively bombed; people could not get out of their cellars for days. It was announced on the radio that on 29 October a corridor would be opened on the Baku-Rostov Highway for those wishing to leave Grozny. People began preparing for the journey, looking for transport.

It was a matter of life and death. My relatives and I decided to go to Nazran along the Baku-Rostov Highway. Chechens call it „the Road of Life", but for many it was to be the Road of Death.

We left on the morning of 29 October. It was a slow drive, and for much of the time we were at a standstill. At about 2.00 pm we crossed the bridge near Shaami-Yurt. Someone told us the Kavkaz checkpoint was closed and they had stopped letting vehicles through. In order not to spend the night on the highway, we decided to go back home and to set off again early the next day. Our attempts to turn back failed: the cars were just packed too closely together, in 4 rows. The column stretched for several kilometres. Motorists were cursing, arguing about who was in the way of whom. A traffic jam built up. Later we found out that there was a Kamaz truck across the road at the end of the column preventing cars from driving back. The column was caught in a trap.

Suddenly, Su-25 attack bombers came whistling overhead. They were flying so low you thought they might slice off the car roofs. We were numb with fear and had no time to jump out of the car. Very nearby we heard explosions. The car shook. Avalu, sitting in the driver's seat, was staring glassily at the exposed bone of his left thigh. The leg slid slowly down. There were pieces of muscle and skin still on the bone and blood was gushing from the stump, flooding the car floor.

„I've been wounded. I've got blood on my chest," Tukhan shouted choking. His face was covered in blood from glass splinters from the shattered windscreen. On the left side of his shirt a huge blood stain was getting bigger. Amnat and I clambered out of the car and began shouting for help.

Nobody came. There was the incessant din of exploding shells, machine-gun fire, the screaming of people beside themselves with fear, the groans and cries of the injured. The bombers kept coming back again and again, annihilating the column before finally flying off. The air was full of groans and screaming, cars were on fire, everything was in turmoil. We began carrying the wounded to the side of the road. Binding Avalu's thigh tightly above the stump with some cloth, Amnat and I dragged him out of the car. He was in critical condition, pale, his features pinched, his face covered with beads of cold, clammy sweat. He was groaning quietly and his breathing was shallow. I felt his wrist for the pulse and could barely detect it, and it was so fast I could not count it.

He was in shock. What should I do? I had no painkillers, no solution for intravenous transfusion. His 2 sons ran up. They had been driving 200-300 meters ahead of us and fortunately were unscathed.

„Bring the car quickly. Avalu urgently needs to be taken to the nearest hospital!"

Tukhan was choking. He had a splinter in his chest. He was sitting in front, next to Avalu. I found a sheet among the belongings in a nearby truck, folded and wound it tightly round his chest several times. We had difficulty pulling him out of the car: in May he had had a stroke and his right arm and leg were not working properly. His wife Seda continued sitting in the back seat. She seemed calm and indifferent to what was happening, but her big, beautiful eyes had a look of fatalism in them.

„Zara, I think I have been hit too," she said, holding her stomach with both hands after we had dragged the men out of the car. I examined her abdomen. There was a small entry wound with ragged edges. There was no external bleeding, and at first glance her condition did not seem critical. I was called away to other people who were injured. I do not remember whom I helped or how, if indeed it can even be called help, without tourniquets, bandages, painkillers, or anti-shock solutions. What has lodged in my memory is the mutilated corpses, severed limbs and heads, blood, screams, the chaos, the ringing in my ears.

We finally managed to arrange for the injured to be taken to nearby hospitals. We took Avalu to one and they dressed the stump, but he died within 2 hours from loss of blood. Tukhan and Seda were given first aid and sent on to Argun. There were so many wounded people. In Urus-

Martan District Hospital they prioritised them, because they did not have enough surgeons, operating theatres or drugs. Injured people whose operations could be postponed for 1 or 2 hours were sent to other towns: Starye Atagi, Argun, or Shali.

I went with my relatives. Tukhan and Seda underwent surgery.

Tukhan died 2 days later, and Seda died unexpectedly 4 days later. No one knows how many were killed that day. It was the only corridor for leaving Chechnya, so there were refugees from every town and village.

Their families took the dead back home for burial, and the injured were examined and sent on all over the place. The members of our family who died are counted as survivors.

Russian army officials at first denied there had been any shooting of refugees, but some days later, after publications in *Novaya Gazeta* and *Moskovskie Novosti*, issued a statement that a column of fighters had been exterminated: „Two trucks carrying militants were destroyed".

I need not have bothered wondering who had given the order to bomb a refugee column. I later learned that, the same day, a convoy of refugees had also been fired at on the Petropavlovskaya Highway. People who survived the initial attack were shot by snipers in hills near the road, while what in Russia passes for an army looted the refugees' cars. This was unquestionably a planned operation to annihilate the civilian population.

„We were ordered to shoot anything that moved, even a baby in a pram!" wounded Russian soldiers admitted during the first war. I do not suppose that in this war they have been ordered to comply with international conventions on the treatment of civilians. General Gennadiy Troshev was commander of the Joint Command of Federal Forces in Chechnya at this time. He should be sitting in the dock in the Hague alongside Milosevic, not writing his memoirs.

The senseless brutality and pathological hatred of the Russians for Chechens which Leo Tolstoy described in his tale, *Hadji-Murad*, has in no way diminished in the intervening 150 years.

I stayed in the village until all my family's funerals were over. I could no longer sleep peacefully. I had only to fall asleep to see the same, invariable scene: that road, the bombers hurtling towards us. As soon as they started firing their missiles I would wake up. I carried sleeping pills with me wherever I went, but they were no help.

The memories that came flooding back made me cry to myself for a long time. Margot and Armen tried to comfort me, to ask questions, but I could not understand what they were saying. I did not want to talk. I took out my sleeping pills and swallowed 3. Without noticing, I was soon asleep after all the exhaustion and emotional stress of the last few days.

The stars disappeared, dawn was breaking. Nearby a cockerel crowed to tell us a new morning had arrived. Once more I am standing in the courtyard of the house in Grozny which I moved back into 1 month before the start of the second war, after 2 years of repairs. The yard is full of plants and there has always been something in flower from early spring till late autumn. I stand there among the roses and a bee is hard at work, collecting nectar. I can just hear him buzzing to himself, maybe grumbling that his life is so hard. Suddenly it seems to me that someone at the gate is following my every move. I listen intently. A bee, a cockerel... But what else? The buzzing and whistling grow louder, the bees' wings grow larger, like those of the car in the French movie „Fantômas".

It is a bomber. Now it is going to start! Someone comes up behind me and takes my hand. Theirs, in a long white sleeve, is cold.

A thought flashes through my mind. „Death, I suppose. No cause for alarm! Here it is, deliverance from all my suffering!" That cold touch wakes me up.

„I do not want to live..."

(Testimony of Ruslan Angaev, Grozny, Sector 9, 29 October 1999. Recorded by the Association of Captives of Filtration Camps in the CRI)

When the war came closer to Grozny and it was no longer possible to stay, I and my family left. Early on the morning of 27 October 1999 we were on the Rostov-Baku Highway, heading towards Shatoy. I was driving and had my whole family in the car with me. In front was an ordinary bus crammed full of passengers. Suddenly, I heard screaming in the car.

My youngest daughter, who was 5, was shrieking at the top of her voice, „Daddy, that plane! I'm frightened ... Daddy!"

At just that moment, the bus in front of us was hit by a shell and ripped in two. There were old people, women and children in it. The planes were firing on the traffic. I was sure this was the end. I stopped the car immediately. We managed to run away from the road and hide among the trees. The next missile hit our car. The blast was so powerful it threw me and my younger daughter against some rocks and injured her leg. She screamed at the top of her voice, drowning out everything and everyone else. I seemed to have lost my mind and it took me a long time to come to my senses, but her mother pressed the child's head to her breast, whispering over and over, „Allah have mercy on us!"

The planes came one after another. They kept flying in and firing at the vehicles on the road. Some managed to jump out of theirs, but others were burned alive in them along with their whole family. The people in the bus were crying out, imploring Allah for help, but the planes kept firing and firing. Each time they flew over they took new lives. People were bleeding. One person had lost an arm, someone else had been hit in the leg, someone had lost both legs, but the planes kept firing and firing at living targets. It went on for half an hour.

„It looks like they have stopped. They seem to have gone," my wife said and we came out of hiding.

People who had just arrived quickly got out of their cars to help the victims. They began pulling people out of the burning bus, those who had survived. Some had been burned to cinders and it was impossible to identify them. Tears were pouring down my face. Nearby lay a human arm, somewhere else the upper part of a woman's body. The lower part had been blown far away. It was a terrible sight: mutilated human bodies, streams of blood collecting in pools. The people who had just driven up were in a hurry to take away the wounded to the nearest hospital in Chiri-Yurt, because the planes might come back.

Somebody took us to that hospital, along with the others. My daughter was bleeding. Her injured right leg was hanging off. My wife was beside herself from the shock, so it fell to me to organise everything.

A lot of maimed people were brought that day to the hospital in Chiri-Yurt, people who had lost limbs, or were wounded and needed surgery. There were many dead people. I do not know how many; there was no time to count. That day will remain in my memory forever.

My 5-year-old daughter had her leg amputated. O, Allah! You cannot imagine how a father suffers for his child, the pain when a tiny person looks at you in tears and asks, „Daddy, my leg! How am I going to play now? And when I see a plane in the sky, how will I run to the basement? Daddy, when is this war going to be over?" She stopped then and fell asleep, worn out by the pain and terrible scenes of the day, when people were being burned alive in a blazing bus or car and no one could pull them out until the planes flew away.

I had the most terrible thoughts. At that moment I regretted ever having had a family and children. I could not bear to see my daughter's pain. What must a 5-year-old feel who has just lost her leg? Oh, Allah!

She should still be playing with dolls, and her lot has been to suffer these terrible trials. It is so early for her to experience the savagery of this unjust world.

„Daddy, I do not want to wake up. I do not want to live!" Her words pierced my heart. I, her father, can do nothing to help her. What is going on? What are these people doing to us? Tell me, what kind of future can a child have if the one thought she has in her mind is, 'I do not want to live'? What am I to do? Help me.

Eyewitness accounts of the bombing of the refugee convoy on October 29, 1999:

Zarita Hamzatovna Saralieva sheltered 11 relatives from the Chechen Republic of Ichkeria in her apartment. On 22 November 1999 they came to the Citizens' Assistance Committee. Zina Hamzatovna Hamidova related the following:

On 28 October, the army promised that the next day between 9.00 and 10.00 am there would be an opportunity to leave Chechnya. By 9 o'clock the column of vehicles and people between Achkhoy-Martan and Shaami-Yurt stretched for 11 kilometres. At 10 o'clock it was announced that people would not be allowed out. Vehicles and people began to disperse. At this moment, 2 planes appeared in the sky. They rose and fell many times and bombed the column. A terrible panic broke out. With Zina

Hamzatovna were her children, her daughter-in-law, her mother and brother. During the bombing 3 members of the Hamidov family were killed. Zina's son, Rustam Hamidov, lost his young pregnant wife, Elona Isaeva, born 1983. They had been married that summer.

Elona kept a diary, from which they learnt she was pregnant. The diary is full of warm words about her relatives. Her brother, Said-Mahomed Isaev, born 1990, was killed with her, and their relative Asma Mahomedova, born 1954. Zina herself was wounded in the arm. According to her testimony, out of 30 people in a nearby truck only 1 person survived.

No one has heard of the pilots being punished for this massacre. The head of the Federal Migration Service in an interview with Svetlana Gannushkina confirmed that these events took place and said an investigation was under way.

Recorded in the Citizens' Assistance Committee, 22.11.1999

The account of Luiza Bakaeva, a refugee from Chechnya

In 1994 when the war began, I was expecting a baby. I was in the ninth month of pregnancy. On 26 November when the bombing started, I was having contractions and was taken to the maternity hospital but there was no one there and I was brought back home. Then on the 29th the bombing started again, and I started bleeding. I was taken to a different hospital and gave birth prematurely on 30 November 1994 In 1994, in late December, my 5-storey apartment block was bombed.

It was by the railway station, next to the KGB and Interior Ministry buildings at No. 1, Ordjonikidze Prospekt, Apartment 31. With 3 children and my youngest son in my arms, I and my husband went back to our village. The baby had thrush in his mouth, nappy rash, and bleeding from the navel. I myself could neither sit nor walk because it had been a difficult birth.

In 1995, when my husband was driving to the city from the village to see how my father and his parents were, he was stopped on the road by armed soldiers who confiscated his Kamaz truck. (Luiza's husband was a driver by profession – *Ed.*)

In 1996, when Russian troops were in Grozny, my grandparents' house was blown up at 23.30. My eldest daughter was there with them and received 65% burns. It was the old New Year's Eve, the night of 13 January. She could not be taken to hospital because there was a curfew.

One of our neighbours, a drug addict, injected her in a vein and that kept her alive until the morning. In the morning she was taken to the burns unit, where they had absolutely no facilities. They changed her dressings under anaesthetic every other day. She died 2 months later, on 13 March, her wedding anniversary. She was 18 and a half.

Then in August the Chechen fighters came back. We were living with friends across from a military unit. On 7 August there was an explosion outside. I heard people shouting in the street, calling for help.

I heard it but did not want to go out. I was sure they had got my husband, but kept my hopes up until the last. When I heard a lot of men stamping about in the courtyard, I opened the door and shouted in my own language, „You have brought me the one thing I was afraid of." My neighbours said, „Stop shouting and bring a cushion and bandages." But he did not hear me, he was lying there like a corpse. Then the neighbours drove him to the hospital through all the bombing.

I was sure he would never recover and only wondered what was to become of me and the children. When they brought him home from hospital the next day I was frankly amazed. Then the neighbours started coming to visit. He tried to stand up to greet one neighbour, a very old man, and re-opened all his wounds. Then our neighbour took us all to his village of Chechen-Aul. My brother came there and took us to Nalchik. He said, „We don't want him rotting in front of everybody." In Nalchik they put him in the hospital. They examined me too and said they were going to put me in the hospital, but I could not go and lie in bed there. I had to go to the hospital twice a day to care for my husband, and I had an 18-month-old baby and 2 children to look after, 1 aged 6 and the other aged 5.When everything settled down again at home, we went back. My husband got a job as a watchman at the dental hospital, where his brother's wife was a dentist. I got my children into a school. We mended the roof, did some plastering, and installed heating in the house we were given to live in. That winter I made jams and pickles like never before, and bought flour. I only had potatoes left to buy, whitewashed the walls, painted the woodwork, and thought we would see in this New Year like normal human beings. This time (i.e., in the autumn of 1999 – *Ed*.) I thought I would not go anywhere, because my father said he was not going out. God forbid anyone should have to choose between their parents and their children.

I could not just leave my parents, not knowing if I would see them again or not, or look my children in the eye, who were waiting for me to come up with some kind of solution.

I grew up in a working class family. My mother was a seamstress and my father a driver, and I never had to envy other people's children, despite the fact that neither of my parents could read or write. Now, though, my children lack everything: good health, good food, good education ... to say nothing of entertainment. I am ashamed to look them in the eye, because I have nothing to give them. But they, especially the older one who is 10, understand that, in spite of all my troubles, I am at least trying to make something out of nothing for them.

We were waiting for them to open the corridor to Ingushetia. Nine days passed. They said they would unblock the border post on 29 October.

That day, we set off for the border at 5.00 am. It was raining and foggy. I had a bad feeling and told my father about it. I said, „Dad, I just do not know what will happen to you at home or what will happen to us on this journey." He said to me, „Nothing can happen to you on the journey: you are refugees." I told him they were bombing refugees, but he said, „That can't be true."

We stayed at the border post until 10.40 am. The soldiers told us they had not received orders today, and the border would not be opened for another 5 days. We asked the soldiers if there was any guarantee we would not get bombed, and they said that for 15 kilometres around them to the left, to the right, and ahead there would be no bombing, but other than that they did not know.

We had driven about 20-25 kilometres when my eldest son said, „Mum, look, there are planes ahead and white steam coming from them.

They are getting ready to bomb." Our neighbour, who we had picked up on the way back (he was walking) said, „Everybody run for the trees!" We all ran and prayed to God to save us from this hell. I had my daughter lying beside, or rather, underneath me; my elder son was being shielded by his father; and the younger was in our neighbour's arms.

After the first attack, my younger son said to our neighbour, „I got hit."

The neighbour did not want me to hear what he had said. He asked, „Where did you get hit?" The little boy said „In my arm." The neighbour looked but his hand did not seem to be bleeding.

Then there was a second raid. Something cracked in my ears and I shouted to our neighbour, „Put your fingers in the child's ears." We went deep into the forest when they started the third raid. The people in cars in front of ours were all killed. The same thing happened to the people in the one behind us: they were killed too. We saw their mangled bodies. When we got back to our car, the windows were broken and the car was all dented. The Almighty came to our aid, it started up, and we drove it to my father's house. He was very shocked. He sat at the table clutching his head in his hands and said, „So, they gave them orders to fire at refugees on the main road."

When we got back, my younger son said, „Mum, I want to have a look at my arm. Can you pull up my sleeves." He had been strong through all this horror and fear. His arm was covered in blood and I had never seen a wound like it. There was something very odd about it. We took him to see a nurse at her home. She sprinkled some yellow powder on his arm. It was all red and swollen.

My husband and children flatly refused to go on that road again, even if they did open the border. After that we walked to the border with Dagestan. From there we went to Gerzel. There was a night train to Moscow. We got on it, came here to stay with a friend and I am still with her.

I ask you to help me and my family, just out of human kindness.

This text was submitted to the Citizens' Assistance Committee on 26 November 1999 as an application for aid.

Firing on the „humanitarian corridor" on Petropavlovskaya Highway on the road to Dagestan, 29 October 1999

Massacre of the Alhazurov family
(of 64 Demian Bednyi Street, Chervlennaya, Shelkovsky Region, Chechnya)
Alhazurov, Sultan Kazhahmetovich, born 18 December 1934, father of the family;
Madueva, Kuzhan Sultanovna, born 1 January 1953, daughter of Sultan;
Madueva, Heda Ihvanovna, born 1987, daughter of Kuzhan;
Maduev, Usman Ihvanovich, born 1986, son of Kuzhan;
Buhaeva, Zarema Alievna, born 1 March 1972, daughter-in-law of Sultan;
Alhazurova, Karina Aslanbekovna, born 19 May 1992, daughter of Zarema;
Alhazurova, Fariza Aslanbekovna, born 13 October 1999, daughter of Zarema.

The account of Koka Alhazurova
(mother of the massacred family, who was not in the refugee convoy)
They were living as refugees in Tauzen in Vedeno District. That day their journey took them home to Chervlennaya in Shelkovsky District.
All the mass media were announcing that a corridor was being provided for refugees. People who regularly listened to the radio and watched television decided to make use of it. That morning, 29 October 1999, they gathered their belongings together and took to the road, the more so because Vedeno District had been subjected to intense bombardment.
I was told afterwards, by a woman who saw it all herself, that their convoy came under fire from long-range artillery from the direction of Vinogradnoye. I was looking for my little granddaughter because I had been told she was still alive. It turned out, though, that it was someone else's granddaughter. Later I was told that all my family had been killed.
I do not remember this woman's name, but she told us all about it.
She saw a shell hit a Lada Samara the color of wet asphalt, and all the people in it were killed. A man was blown out of the car and called for help, afraid that the petrol tank would explode and burn the bodies, but

there was no one to help. There was constant sniper fire, and even helicopters firing cannon, picking off the survivors.

Another man, who was lucky to stay alive in that hell, told me there were 17 shrapnel fragments in his body. „I evidently only survived because the day appointed for my death by God had not come," he said.

„I was lying to one side, but could clearly hear the groans of the dying and injured." When that man called for help, a woman came to him and he asked her what was happening and what might come next. She replied that we were being murdered, massacred. „Father, we cannot help you at all. Save yourself if you can. I have lost some of my family here myself," she said.

That woman had lost her 2 daughters and husband. She said her husband got shrapnel in his heart from the shell that hit my husband's car.

He was going to the aid of his daughter when our car blew up. That was how he died. They were the Emiev family from Argun.

People from Tolstoy-Yurt (Doykar-Evl) gathered up the dead and wounded, as well as those lucky enough not to have been hurt. They took them to the village, and from there to hospitals in Mozdok and Znamenskoye.

There was another woman called Dagoy. Her only son died there that day. She witnessed his death. Her daughter-in-law was left crippled for life. She lost 1 leg and also her 9-year-old son. Their surname was Saidov. They were from Argun too.

The villagers from Tolstoy-Yurt later buried the bodies of 4 of my children: my daughter, Kuzhan; her 2 children, Heda and Usman; and my daughter-in-law, Zarema. They told me that was on 14 November.

Half my granddaughter Heda's body was missing, the upper part. (Their bodies were released 2 weeks after their deaths, but even then we were still unaware of the tragedy. The others simply disappeared. No one knows where they are buried.)

Question: When did you find the bodies of the other people who died, and where did you bury them?

Answer: We tried to get the burials excavated for many long months.

It happened only 7 months later, on 3 June 2000. That day we went to Goryachevodsk. The burial site was in the courtyard of an asphalt plant near the village. The pit was huge, the size of a house. When they excavated it they found 7 bodies and 4 vehicles, 1 of which was a truck. The bodies were under the vehicles.

They started excavating at 11 o'clock. There were several army people there. One of them was the deputy district prosecutor, another was the prefect, and there was the head of the village administration. They helped us a lot. There were other people too who, like us, were looking for their loved ones from Argun and Petropavlovskaya. They brought an excavator to do the digging, and a crane, because otherwise it would have been impossible to get the cars out of the pit. After they had pulled several cars out they found the bodies of 2 girls from Argun. More precisely, 1 was a young pregnant woman. Then they dug up the body of the only son of Dagoy from Argun. Then they dug out our car, and then the bodies of my granddaughters ... *(Koka Alhazurova's story is interrupted because she breaks down in floods of tears. Five minutes or so later, when she has composed herself, she continues her story, despite the distress it is causing her.)*

Q: Did you see the bodies being recovered from the pit? What state were they in?

A: Yes, I looked and saw this terrible scene. I don't suppose I will ever forget that mutilated baby in nappies. His little body had been smashed. I could see only the skull in the nappies. The other, a sevenyearold girl, had been decapitated. She had been hit by a shell. Her skull was lying next to her. I saw her shoulders and noticed her right arm was missing, but she was still wearing the sweater she had had on.

It was so horrible. These were my granddaughters who had never done anyone any harm. After they had brought up their little bodies, the soldiers said there would not be time to get the others out; they had been in that pit for 7 months and 1 more night would make no difference. We would have to wait until tomorrow morning. As often still happens, though, by the next morning the Russian agencies had changed their minds. When we arrived at the factory courtyard it was as if the whole army had turned up, cordoned off the pit and would not let us anywhere near it. You would have thought we had come to commit an act of sabotage or recover the bodies of Chechen fighters. The soldiers had dogs with them, and there were a great many of them. At that moment the prefect of the district arrived with the Russian commandant and it as only after they intervened that we were allowed to continue the exhumation.

On the morning of 4 June, we recovered 2 more bodies out of the pit: 1 was the body of my husband and the other no one could identify.

He was buried in Tolstoy-Yurt unidentified. The truth of the matter is that some of the Russian soldiers felt sorry for us, and some were even in tears, but we were not allowed to take a photo of the bodies or the pit.

When my daughter tried to photograph the burial site, the officer in charge wagged his finger at her and said they would close off the pit.

After that, she did not try to take any more pictures. My husband's brother photographed his body only when we were at the cemetery. Sultan's body, that is what my husband was called, had no wounds but his head was severely damaged.

For a long time we did not know what had happened to them. We supposed they were with our relatives in Tauzen. But quite by chance, my daughter, who is married, was walking with her husband's family in a convoy of about 100 people on that road on 31 October. She saw her father's wrecked car and rushed over to it, but felt ill. Her brother-in-law and his wife immediately pulled Malkan, my daughter, away from the car. They had been strictly warned on the road not to go near or even look in the direction of the wrecked cars and dead people the Russians had not yet got round to removing. They were told, „If you take 1 step in that direction, we will shoot. Do not even dare to look over there." They did not have time to see whether there was anyone in the car because the windows were darkened. When she later came home, she told us that on 29 October she had gone to the relatives our family had been staying with, but they had already left that morning and the others decided they would leave too. My daughter went on to say that a convoy of refugees had been massacred that morning on the Petropavlovskaya Highway. I expressed concern that our people might have been among them, but she replied that she had heard her father had gone to Nazran. We hoped that was right, but it was impossible to go and find out what had happened because the roads were all sealed off.

We heard what had happened a month later. On 8 December our relatives sent us a message to say that on 29 October they had seen our family off on their way. They asked us to let them know whether or not they had arrived. I was not told about this message, though even people outside our family knew about it. My daughter-in-law went with my neighbour Aizan to Mozdok and went round all the hospitals and other places they thought they might be, in search of our family members.

Their efforts were fruitless.

At this time a woman in a local train asked for the relatives of Sultan from Chervlennaya to be informed that everybody had been killed near Tolstoy-Yurt, the whole family who had been in a Samara the colour of wet asphalt. That is how we did in the end find out what had happened.

When we got this message, the wife of my brother-in-law went to Tolstoy-Yurt to see what more she could find out. She managed to discover that 4 of the 7 bodies were buried in Tolstoy-Yurt: Kuzhan, her 2 children and Zarema. The upper part of the girl's body was missing: they had buried only the lower part. It was not known where the other 3 were.

By now it was already December.

In March, my second daughter, Malika, died in hospital in Arkhangelsk after hearing about the deaths in our family. The doctor said that she had had an acute reaction to the stress. She was ill because of what happened, did not have long to live, and it would be best for her to be taken home. My daughter Malkan was not able to do that, and how could she have told her sister she had not long to live? Malika died on 14 March.

Malkan brought her back 5 days later, and she was buried on 20 March. She had been a journalist before the war.

It was only 2 months after Malika died that we found and buried her father and 2 nieces, as I have already described, on 4 June in Tolstoy-Yurt, only in a different cemetery. My daughter, Kuzhan, and daughterin-law, Zarema, were buried in a single grave; Heda and Usman, Kuzhan's children, in another one; Zarema's children, my granddaughters Karina and Fariza, in another; and Sultan and the unidentified man together in another.

Oh, yes. Before the war, we sold a Gazelle van for 60,000 rubles and my husband was travelling in my son's Lada Samara. We had spent a little of the money, but he had more than 50,000 rubles with him. Afterwards, our relatives told us he had wrapped the money in a sheet along with some other papers: his army service ID, employment records, except for his passport and the documentation for the car. During the exhumation we found the torn sheet but there was neither money nor documents in it. Neither were there any of the documents he had kept on him, not even torn or burned. The documents and the money had simply disappeared.

The account of Laila Alhazurova

(Koka's daughter)

I saw a young soldier talking to some of the local lads at the market in Chervlennaya. He was telling them how the soldiers had been forced to shoot a refugee column on 29 October 1999. They were firing at civilians who were driving towards Shelkovsky District. He said that when they tried to protest that there were women, old people and children in the column, their commander told them: „There is an order, issued by our superiors, and orders must be obeyed unconditionally."

He said to these young people with tears in his eyes, „How can I live with myself now? I go to sleep and I see these women and children and old people in my dreams. I hear their screams and groans, their cries for help, even though that day I saw them only through binoculars. I will never forget this."

I did not know when he was talking that my husband's family had been killed in that column.

The account of Rizwan Ahmetovich Didaev, born 1949

I, Rizwan Ahmetovich Didaev, a resident of Staraya Sunzha, together with my family, drove on to the Petropavlovskaya Highway on 29 October 1999 to go to Ingushetia. On the way, we were joined by my sister's family. People had told us that on 29 October a corridor would be provided for those wishing to leave for other regions of Russia. Of course, we decided to take advantage of it. On the way, a whole convoy of vehicles formed of people who, like us, were leaving for safer areas. We hung out white flags and set off. Later there was a sharp bend in the road to the left. In front of us was my sister's car with her brother-in-law at the wheel. When I turned our car into the bend, I could not understand what had happened. A first shell hit my sister's car. A second exploded near mine, sending up a pillar of dust, and debris rained down on us. We were second in the convoy and I decided to hit the accelerator and drive fast through the hills, but when I drove on round the bend I saw a smashed truck in front of me and people lying in the road. I could not tell at the time whether they were alive or dead. Another shell exploded and I shouted to everyone to get out of the car and lie on the ground. When I got out, I saw an overturned Volga saloon, and later learned that this was the car of our friends from Tolstoy-Yurt. At the time, though, I had no idea what was happening. Near one car a concussed man was standing, also totally bewildered. All this time snipers were firing: „ping – ping". I still have that sound in my ears. At this point, the concussed man walked past his own car, saw mine and got in. It occurred to me that the keys were still in it, but I could not make up my mind what to do next.

There was another explosion, after which he got out, slammed the door, and walked off down the road. I do not know his name, but he could not have told me it himself. (When he was at the hospital in the evening, he kept trying all the time to leave: they would bring him back and he would go off again.) There was dust everywhere, smoke, people screaming.

Somebody shouted that the children and Usman had been killed. When everyone had got out of the car, we all slipped into the drainage ditch and crawled to Goryachevodsk. I have been driving along this road for a long time and know it well, and the ditch too. We crept along it for 3 or 3 and a half kilometres. It was not safe to raise your head because snipers were firing constantly, but you still wanted to take a look after each explosion.

As I crawled along, I counted about 30 wrecked cars. Not one drove past us. They had chosen the time and place for the shooting very carefully: the road along which a refugee column would have to pass; the day when a corridor for refugees had been declared. They were firing directly at every vehicle. I even said those tank crews should get top marks for the accuracy of their targeting. If a shell only landed nearby, the driver could stop the car and children would pour out on to the road. In most cases, though, they scored a direct hit. It was a hideous scene, shrapnel, wounded people, and against that background you glimpsed the angel faces of little children.

We were being fired at every instant, explosions thundering, shells exploding.

We were in the ditches, and the moment you raised your head you were likely to be hit.

There were so many bodies, lumps of human flesh scattered about, arms, legs, heads, bits of torsos. I saw all this with my own eyes, because I kept raising my head and looking out, even though my wife was scolding me. When we came to a corner, we needed to move across to the other side. I suggested they should run across one by one, even though we knew the federals were watching and could see everyone through their binoculars. Others objected, and we decided to wait for darkness to fall By this time, the head of the Goryachevodsk village administration had managed to negotiate with those commanding the federals to give them an opportunity to take people away from the scene. They gave an hour and a half to 2 hours for the villagers to help the victims. The first car to leave Tolstoy-Yurt picked us up near Goryachevodsk, along with a few other people who, like us, had been crawling towards the village. Another truckload of young people came out to collect the injured and dead bodies.

They told us later that after they had collected 5 bodies the firing started again, shooting near the wheels of their car as if to tell them to get a move on. At this time a bus and several more cars arrived, another small column. They too loaded people in and got through. They were not bombarded, although there was sniper fire. The federals presumably decided not to fire at them because they wanted them to do their work quickly.

There was 1 seriously injured woman. The doctor gave her an injection immediately and worked on her wound. She was a healthy woman.

Her fist was clenched, and her whole body was covered in shrapnel wounds, and the right side of her face. The injection evidently did not help. They carried her a hundred meters or so, but did not make it to the hospital before she died. (I think she was from Vedeno.)

They sent the rest of us off in a group to Tolstoy-Yurt, because it was not safe to stay in Goryachevodsk. They ferried the wounded by car, and we walked.

My sister and niece were brought there 2 days later.

Some of the wounded were sent to Mozdok: among them was an Uzbek woman who was travelling from Argun. She is married to the cousin of my father-in-law. She had her daughter's son with her and 2 grandsons, the children of her son, and she had a note for Walid Israilov.

I was told he was our brother.

Five children and a 28-year old woman wandered around these hills for 5 days. They told us the little girl said, „If I got home right now, I would eat 10 cakes and drink 10 glasses of water." They did their best to comfort her. After their 5-day travels they came to the village. Two of the Ozdamirovs' boys were wounded.

Testimony of Elman Gataev

(from the website www.invalid.nm.ru)

On 29 October 1999, I left Argun to reach my parents and relatives in a village. You could expect „precision-guided" bombing almost anywhere.

In spite of that I thought I would get away with it, but when our car drove into Tolstoy-Yurt, 3 planes appeared above us. At first they just flew over us, then they started making runs, as if they were going to fire, making us really panic. In fact, though, after giving us a fright,

they flew off. We had barely breathed a sigh of relief when, suddenly, there were 2 more planes which started bombing us and the village we were near.

When I regained consciousness, our car was burned out and there was a smell of burnt flesh. After lying for a long time on the ground, I started shivering and felt a severe pain in my right foot. I crawled a short way from where I was to under a tree by the roadside. I sat up and was going to take off my shoe, but found that my leg just above the shoe was barely hanging on by the skin. Evidently I had been hit too. I tightly bandaged my leg just above the wound to stop the bleeding and began crawling towards the village.

I do not know how far I crawled, but it seemed an eternity. I heard shouting and wailing. It was the villagers who had waited for the planes to fly off after firing all their ammunition. They ran out to the road in the hope of saving people. One woman hauled me up on her back and half carried, half-dragged me to the hospital. She did at least manage to take me to the place they called a hospital, but it was a half-ruined, empty building.

They gave me first aid of sorts.

Very few people had survived. Several children were howling because their mothers had been killed. Women were weeping over their dead children, wives over their husbands. The men stood, their heads bowed, silently looking at this dreadful scene. Everyone knew a terrible wrong had been committed by the Kremlin, but nobody could do anything about it. Each accepted their fate.

The story of a victim who declined to give their name

On 29 October I was driving from Argun, transporting refugees. Near Tolstoy-Yurt our column was hit by heavy artillery from where federal troops were deployed. I had started going downhill, came round a bend, and saw a black car on fire. Beyond it were several other burning cars.

I was just about to put my foot on the accelerator to make a run for the village when my vehicle was hit.

A Lada Samara the color of wet asphalt drove up behind. We yelled, „Drive as fast as you can!" but they were evidently confused, stopped, and suffered a direct hit. I do not think anybody survived, and there were at least 6 people in it.

Another 4 people from a different car were killed on the spot. The rest were all covered in shrapnel wounds, lying in blood until it was dark. It was impossible to get away from there. There was no let-up in the bombardment, with heavy artillery firing at vehicles, and snipers picking off the survivors.

Only 3 cars raced through. About 27 vehicles, cars and trucks, were wrecked. I doubt whether anyone in a saloon car survived: in the trucks, maybe.

The meadow was strewn with the living and the dead, out in the rain. We waited for darkness in the hope of somehow crawling away; the shelling did not let up for a minute. They just went on and on firing, and you thought something was bound to land on you. Snipers were firing from the hill behind Vinogradnoye. Several times bullets flew just over your head. You had only to look up a little and they would fire.

There were 27 of us in the vehicle: my own and my brother's family.

Five people were killed and all the others were wounded. The bodies of Zara Ismailova and Malika Emieva were left in their car and were later dragged away together with it by the federals. They were about 25 years old. They were friends.

After the 29th, we were taken from there to hospital, where I went to see a relative, Mahomed Abubakarov. He was lying there with a drip attached. One side of his body was completely shattered. I went and said a couple of words and Mahomed recognised me. I asked him how he had got there. The next morning the doctor came out and said, „It's over. He's died."

Nuresh's account

They would not allow anyone through. As soon as you came near they would immediately fire. I grabbed them by the hand, those bastards. I had no other options. My whole family were dying there. I begged them for help. I walked there, as far as the Terek, to Komsomol Bridge. They said, „Give us 1,000 rubles and you can go through on foot." Of course I did not have 1,000 rubles! I cried and cried. Sharapov was our commandant at that time. I hugged him. I hate him, but I had come to the end of my tether. I said, „Help me, please. My son is there almost dead, and all my family are there. Give me a car, or a permit. Anything!"

On the third day he gave me a car and his deputy as an escort and I went to collect them.

I brought them back then. How much I had to pay! They were all in hospital ill, all of them covered in blood. One had their head all cut, another their leg. My son is still full of shrapnel. I brought back 2 of Laila's grandchildren who had survived, and her daughter-in-law. They were all covered in blood. I thought the wound on the face of one of them could never heal. Zara Abdulkarimova was in that car – she was 9 months pregnant – and her 2 unmarried sisters, Daresh and Umani.

The rest of the bodies they just buried using an excavator. Local people saw what they did. Recently some women went there and found at the site children's shorts, an arm, pieces of dresses sticking out. There are still traces there today. From that piece of a dress it is obvious there is something else there. Women's hair has been found. They wrote tosome commander and said, „Give us our dead. This is unacceptable for us. There has to be a grave." They replied at that time, „We have no sappers, and the bodies might be booby-trapped." Our women responded, „We can find sappers for you. Let us at least do something." He finds a variety of different reasons for refusing. Or perhaps he is on the lookout for a lot of money or something else. Our relatives from Argun have gone there 5 times. It is all just chaotic.

A family was killed there: Hasen Emiev, the father, he had just retired; his daughter, Madina, 29, the eldest; his second daughter, Malika, 21. Both were unmarried, just girls. They have found nothing, not legs, no body, nothing. They found one of the father's legs after 10-12 days.

The Abdulkarimov family: the mother, Padam, and her daughter, Daresh; the second daughter, Umani; the third daughter, Zara. They had no father. Zara was pregnant. She tied all the money they had to her girdle, 25,000 rubles. They thought a pregnant woman would not be searched. Zara was killed, and Padam. When Umani saw this terrible scene she ran away with some other people's children. There were 4 children. They went right up into the mountains. For 4 days they drank rainwater and ate grass like cattle. They hid in a pipe and a ditch to avoid being caught. A sniper kept shooting at them. They were barefoot, without warm clothing, barely alive. They were found on the fifth day. She had such a cold she could not even talk. She is just 19.

The little one was 2 years old and sitting in the cabin of the truck with Laila. Their mother ran into the field and perished there. I brought back these 2 children and their mother and 1 daughter, but 3 children were already dead. I also brought back the mother of my daughter-in-law, and 1 daughter, but now the doctors say they will have to take off one of her arms. We took her immediately to Mozdok, straight from there, 1 daughter. One side of her body looked as if it had been beaten with a hammer, she lost so much blood. They spent 13,000 rubles in Mozdok, but even now she is half dead. They recently went back to Argun but there is nothing there either to eat or drink.

All they possessed they were taking in that car. My son needs to undergo a medical examination for disability benefits and I have no money. God forbid anyone should ever see such a nightmare again.

God forbid!

Intestines, heads on the road, arms and legs, blood flowed as if it had been pouring with rain. For heaven's sake, they could see the white flags, they could see it was refugees. They saw it all clearly! How could anyone do something like that? All of them just poor people, and almost all of them massacred. And now people are still searching for their loved ones. Everybody is crying, blundering about, not even half have been found yet. They don't yet know anything.

List of those killed during the firing on a refugee convoy near Tolstoy-Yurt, 29 October 1999

1. Didaeva, Leyla, 40, Severnyi State Farm, Naur District;
2. Karsanov, Ruslan, 38;
3. Abubakarov, Usman, born 1976;
4. Abubakarov, Mahammad, born 1966;
5. Aliev, Arbi;
6. Emieva, Madina, born 1970, Argun;
7. Emieva, Malika, born 1976;
8. Emiev, Hasan, 80;
9. Saidov, Ilman, 8;
10. Saidov, Ibrahim, 44, permission to collect the body withheld;
11. Abakaeva, Zargan, 59, Chernokozovo;

12. Vaduev, Sultan, 75, Tolstoy-Yurt;
13. Maidaev, Sharani, 90, Argun;
14. Maidaev, Husen, 10;
15. Temirgaev, Abubakar, 27, Kalinovskaya;
16. Abdulkarimova, Zara, body not found;
17. Abdulkarimova, Daresh, body not found;
18. Batmurzaev, Abdul-Kosum, born 1936, Petropavlovskaya, body not found;
19. Alhazurov, Sultan, 66, Chervlennaya;
20. Alhazurova, Zarema, 27, daughter-in-law of Sultan Alhazurov;
21. Alhazurova, Karina, 8, daughter of Zarema Alhazurova;
22. Alhazurova, Fariza 1 month, youngest daughter of Zarema Alhazurova;
23. Mudaeva, Kuzhan, 53;
24. Mudaeva, Heda, 13, daughter of Kuzhan Mudaeva;
25. Mudaev, ?, 10, son of Kuzhan Mudaeva;
26. Isa (surname unknown).

List of wounded during the firing on a refugee convoy near Tolstoy-Yurt, 29 October 1999

1. Nasuhanov, Yusup, born 1978, Chernokozovo;
2. Gatsaev, Hamid, 45 years, Postnyi Farmstead;
3. Saidova, Lyuba, born 1966, Argun;
4. Saidova, Leyla, 6;
5. Saidova, Zargan, 3 months;
6. Saidov, Sultan, 4;
7. Saidova, Tamara, 55;
8. Emiev, Umar, 33;
9. Madaeva, Birlant, 40;
10. Ozdamirov, Usman, 12;
11. Ozdamirov, Aslan, 14;
12. Ozdamirova, Lena, 75 (died);
13. Dalaeva, Yaha, 39, Argun;
14. Londamirova, Lena, 31, Chervlennaya;
15. Yasaeva, Lomani, 38, Severnyi State Farm;
16. Hatueva, Malika, 47;
17. Geraev, Kazbek, 73, Kalinovskaya;
18. Emieva, Habila, 47, Argun;
19. Emiev, ?, 3;
20. Emiev, Ibrahim, 32;
21. Abdulkerimova, ?, 28;
22. Abdulkerimova, ?, 60;
23. Chermohanova, Aset, 62;
24. Musiev, Balavdi, 30, Komsomolskoye;
25. Ulubaev, Abdul-Shahid, 76, Lenin Soviet Farm;

26. Ulubaev, ?, 16;
27. Ulubaeva, ?, 19;
28. Abubakarov (died at the hospital).

List of persons missing after the firing on a refugee convoy near Tolstoy-Yurt, 29 October 1999

1. Dalaeva, Shena, 32, Argun;
2. Dalaev, Umar, 15, son of Shena Dalaeva;
3. Dalaev, Moh'mad, 11, son of Shena Dalaeva;
4. Dalaev, Usman, 13, son of Shena Dalaeva;
5. Dalaev, Um-Ela, 8, son of Shena Dalaeva;
6. Dalaeva, Hami, 5, daughter of Shena Dalaeva.

Records of accounts by eyewitnesses from Tolstoy-Yurt, Goryachevodsk, and of interviews of refugees by a staff member of Memorial Human Rights Centre, 28–30 May 2000

A convoy of refugees travelling from Argun towards Naur and Shelkovsky Districts was fired on by federal troops using long-range artillery from the direction of Vinogradnoye, not far from a water pumping station popularly referred to as the Waterworks. The shelling began from 9.00 am and continued without respite for several hours.

Nobody from the villages of Tolstoy-Yurt or Goryachevodsk was allowed to assist these people crazed with fear and horror at what was taking place.

In spite of everything, the head of the village administration of Goryachevodsk managed to negotiate for local residents to be allowed through to help women and children who did not know where to run, where to seek help. Then, at 1.00 pm, a Gazelle van picked up people still on the road who had managed to crawl out from under fire. Next was a ZIL truck with young people from Tolstoy-Yurt who drove directly to the field where the bombardment was taking place.

If there are some discrepancies in the interviews, this is entirely understandable because each interviewee related what they had personally seen and experienced.

The account of a resident of Tolstoy-Yurt who chose not to give his name

The picture became clear when people were brought to the hospital.

Four people died immediately. In the evening a child aged 9 died, as did an old woman the following morning. They were buried in the local cemetery. There were, however, large numbers of wounded. The doctors were unable to cope with all of them. By agreement with the federal troops, a lot of wounded were taken to Znamenskoye. Many had limbs amputated, shrapnel removed, but there was a shortage of medical supplies.

Local people brought what they could to the hospital: bandages, syringes, cotton wool, iodine, etc. Also food and clothing.

One man had lost his children. I do not remember exactly, but think they were found only 4 days later. They had been out in the open for 4 days, hiding from the shooting and not knowing where to go.

The account of Isa from Goryachevodsk

Of the firing at the column on 29 October I remember that artillery fire was heard after 9 o'clock in the morning. Then it somehow became clear that the target was a convoy of refugees trying to leave along the Petropavlovskaya Highway. We tried to go to the aid of people suffering

catastrophically but were not allowed anywhere near where the firing was taking place. We were shot at by snipers. My father managed with great difficulty to get permission to take people away from the bombardment.

The federal troops gave us 2 hours in which to help people, but the snipers did not stop firing. A ZIL truck with lads from Tolstoy-Yurt drove to the field where there were people killed and wounded, as well some lucky enough to be uninjured.

People without cars also came to help and brought out those who had not been injured. Of those who were taken by car, 20 were injured, and there were the same number of dead bodies. About 7 more people died of their wounds at the hospital. As far as I can tell, of those rescued

from the field that day, 25 died. Some of them were buried in Tolstoy-Yurt cemetery. These were people from Argun, Naurskaya and Shelkovskaya. Some were collected by relatives and buried at home. I remember a woman who had lost a leg. Her son was very unwilling to part with her when she was to be taken to the hospital. It was difficult to persuade him that she needed urgent medical help.

Zurab Hasulbekov excelled in assisting the people. At the beginning of October when our village was shelled, his 18-year old wife was killed and his sister, who was 12, was almost ripped to pieces.

The lad who was driving the ZIL truck that day died 6 months later, on 2 April 2000. He was shot dead, almost point blank, on the outskirts of the village when he was driving home that evening. They claimed he had violated the curfew, although it was not even 8 o'clock when his body was collected. His name was Said-Mahomed Shamsuevich Hasuev.

He was born in 1972.

Tremendous help was given to these people also by Ayub Deniev, D. Madaev, Alihan Aliev, Hamzat Hasuhanov, Isa Hasuev and others.

They were firing from long-range artillery and tanks. There were no aircraft. The helicopters were only firing machine guns. As far as I know, 4 children were killed that day.

The account of Mamed

(a villager from Tolstoy-Yurt who was injured that morning and went to the aid of victims at 1.00 pm)

On 29 October at 8.00 in the morning I and my uncle, Sultan Vaduev, left Tolstoy-Yurt to go to Grozny to collect the body of my uncle Salekh Batalov, born 1933, who was killed near his home in Grozny on 27 October during an air raid. It was announced that on 29 October a corridor for refugees wishing to leave particularly dangerous areas of Chechnya would be opened for 4 days and people would be free to leave. I and my uncle, who was born in either 1942 or 1943, drove to the village outskirts, asked whether we could travel to Grozny, and drove on.

Near the water pumping station, long-range artillery opened fire on us. A shell hit our car and threw it 15 meters. It somersaulted 2 or 3 times and stopped. I crawled out and dragged my uncle clear. A piece of shrapnel had gone through his head. I did not want his body burned if the car caught fire. I went back to the road and stopped a car which had been behind us, and returned to the village because we were prevented from taking my uncle's body.

Around 1 o'clock the head of our local administration came to ask for help. I had a ZIL-131 truck and we drove out in it. After the morning's experience I was in no state to drive and my friend, Said-Mahomed Hasuyev, took the wheel. He was killed a month ago. Six or 7 lads volunteered to come and help people. We did not yet know what was going on there. When we came to the road, something terrible was being done. The road and field were littered with dead and wounded people. Mangled vehicles.

People who had fled in panic were lying all over the field under intense fire. We collected the dead and wounded, and people who were uninjured themselves ran to the truck. Bringing everyone we could in the time, we took them to the hospital in Tolstoy-Yurt. Among the wounded were maimed children who had lost arms, legs. Many of those murdered were buried in the local cemetery. My uncle, Sultan Vaduev, was buried there too. We collected and buried the body of Salekh Batalov only later, on 8 November. The federal troops looted all the vehicles wrecked that day.

For several days afterwards they did not allow anyone near. It became evident that they had been sanitising the scene of their crimes.

The account of Ramzan Bolatbiev, mullah of Tolstoy-Yurt, who officiated at the funerals of those killed that day

I officiated at the funerals of the people massacred during the shelling of 29 October 1999. We buried them on 30-31 October, and 2 more some 14 days later when the federal troops handed over their bodies. The names known to us are written on the monuments on the graves. I do not, of course, remember now how many people we buried, but it was about 15 or 16. Some were buried with 2 in the same grave. You can find out more about that at the cemetery. I also remember that the bodies of 3 people were taken by their relatives directly from the hospital. I was told, though, that several more bodies were taken the next day. There were also people who died later from their wounds, and not only in the hospital in Tolstoy-Yurt but in others they were moved to that day.

In the cemetery some friends or family members were buried 2 to a grave because people did not have the strength to dig so many graves at the same time. In 2 days, 16 people were buried here.

Emiev, Hasen, born 1940;
Emieva, Madina, born 1970, buried in the same grave;
Abubakarov, Mahomed, born 1966;
Aliev, Arbi, born 1972, buried in the same grave;
Saidov, Ilman, born 1991;
Maidaev, Shaaran, born 1914;
Maidaev, Husein, born 1990, buried in the same grave;
Madueva, Kuzhan Sultanovna, born 1953;
Buhaeva, Zarema Alievna, born 1972, buried in the same grave;
Aliev, Ruslan, born 1955;
Madueva, Heda Ihvanovna, born 1987;
Maduev, Usman Ihvanovich, born 1986, buried in the same grave;
One man, unidentified.

The account of Toita Hasenovna Emieva, born 1974, resident of Argun, travelling with the refugee convoy to Kalinovskaya

On 29 October, I was in a column of refugees on the way to Tolstoy-Yurt. When the shelling of Argun began, we decided to move to a liberated area where military operations had already ceased and it had been announced that „lawful authority" had been established. Collecting together all my possessions, I, together with Kazbek Geraev who was returning home to Kalinovskaya, set off in his truck at 8.00 am on 29 October. It had been announced that that day a refugee corridor was being opened for those who wished to leave dangerous areas of the republic. There were 27 of us on board a GAZ-53 high-sided truck.

At the turning on to the Petropavlovskaya Highway, we stopped and waited for other vehicles to catch up. There were 5-6 vehicles in the convoy, and others arrived. We hung out white strips (flags). The first vehicle to move off was a Lada and we followed it. After we drove into a bend round a hill, we saw that the front vehicle was on fire. As it turned out, the driver had been killed instantly. His wife, Lyuba, who is Russian by birth, lost a leg. Their son, Ilman, also had his legs torn off and died in hospital. He is buried in the Tolstoy-Yurt cemetery. Their 4-month-old daughter was thrown clear of the car. She was found later and, thanks be to Allah, was unharmed. This turned out to be the family of Ibrahim Saidov, whose body has not been found to this day. It is said they buried them somewhere around there.

A shell hit the side of our truck, immediately killing my sister Malika. I saw that myself. My second sister, Madina, was severely injured and died there. We jumped out of the truck and lay on the ground wherever we could. You could not raise your head because snipers were shooting and shells exploding continuously. I and my brother Umalt had our eardrums burst (in my left ear and my brother's right ear). To this day I have 2 pieces of shrapnel in my left wrist that just cannot be removed. Only yesterday I had an operation on that hand and it could not be located. Umalt was wounded in his shoulder, neck and face. My mum, Habira Emieva, born 1947 (also known as Laila) had multiple shrapnel wounds all over her body. So far, they have been able to remove only 1 fragment.

My father ran to the truck to get his daughters. He managed to remove Madina from it, but when he stood up to remove Malika's body he was hit by shrapnel from a shell which exploded behind him. One fragment hit him in the leg, and another, as it turned out, struck him in the heart. He barely managed to crawl back to us and said to my mother, „Do you know what has happened to your daughters?" He was silent for a moment, then asked how his grandson was. He had wounds to his left arm and face. Mum told him not to raise his head because the snipers were firing constantly. He lowered his head and never raised it again.

I saw every vehicle that turned on to the highway suffering the same fate as ours. It was absolutely clear that they were being directly targeted. At least 30 vehicles, and I can say this with full confidence, were wrecked and set on fire. Some were consumed by flames together with the people in them. Altogether, I know, there were 28 bodies. Some were buried in Tolstoy-Yurt and some were taken away by relatives. Some of the bodies have not been found to this day. There is a burial site, but they do not allow it to be opened, although every month they gather people and say they are going to open it, but then find some excuse to put it off till „a better time". None of us know where exactly the site is.

After a few hours, a ZIL-131 appeared on the field and they shouted to us to run to it if we could. There were 5 or 6 people in the truck and they very quickly picked up the dead and wounded. They collected people from the whole of the field, even though snipers were firing all the time. My mum even shouted to them to leave us and not risk their lives, but those lads helped us, they saved our lives and also the bodies of our dead. If it had not been for them, we could not have buried our relatives.

Three members of our family were murdered that morning: our father, Hasen Emiev, born 1940, my sister Madina, born 1970, are buried in a single grave in Tolstoy-Yurt thanks to these people I am talking about.

We were given back the body of my second sister, Malika, born 1978, only 14 days later, and it too is buried in Tolstoy-Yurt. (Author's note: it turned out that the girl buried 2 weeks later was not, in fact, Malika, whose body was found on 3 June 2000 and buried in Tolstoy-Yurt on 4 June. At the time this interview was given, this was not known, which is why the author has this inaccuracy in her account). We are immensely grateful to those people who gave us such invaluable help.

Having loaded the truck, they drove at top speed to save us from the shells and bullets. We were taken to the hospital in Tolstoy-Yurt. Then another vehicle, a Niva off-roader, arrived with more wounded. We were bandaged there, operated on, some people were sent on to Znamenskoye or Mozdok. The bodies of those murdered that they managed to retrieve were buried on 30-31 October at the local cemetery, as I've already said.

We had set off that day with all our possessions, which all vanished without trace. All our gold items (of all the sisters) were with Malika.

They stripped her body even of the boots. To get her back, we stated that all the gold on her they could keep as a ransom for her body. What else could we do? It was 2 weeks before they let us have her body. She was buried in our absence by the people who sheltered us and looked after us for 12 days. I remember the name of the lady. It was Tamara.

As far as I remember, Lena was also killed that day. She was an Uzbek, married to a Chechen. She is buried at the Kalinovskaya State Farm. Two of her grandsons, Aslan and Usman Ozdamirov, were wounded.

Another grandson, Adam, spent several days in the open with other children. Aset and Yaha Cheremhanov were wounded too. As I have mentioned, the Saidovs, both father and son, were killed. Lyuba Saidova lost a leg. She was transferred to hospital in Mozdok. We were all in a state of shock.

On the night of 29 October, young villagers brought back a Gazelle van with 5 bodies.

We were not bombed by aircraft. There was only shelling from long-range artillery and tanks. There were helicopters circling above us, but they did not launch missiles, only fired their machine guns.

The account of Umani Abdulkerimova

(born 1971, daughter of Alpatu Abdulkerimova, lived with her mother in Argun)

When the shell hit the truck, something struck the back of my head and I lost consciousness for a time. When I came to, I realised I had not been knocked out for long. There were dead bodies next to me, then I saw that one of them belonged to my sister. As I jumped out of the truck, I wondered about the driver. It occurred to me that if he was dead we would not be able to get away. It had not yet occurred to me that whatever happened we were not going to be able just to leave. Thank God, though, the driver was still alive, although he had been wounded. The shells carried on exploding around us and bullets were whistling. I just ran for my life to get away from this hell. I stopped to get my breath and saw 6 children next to me. We hid from the snipers in a ditch, but there was no escape that way. Getting out of the ditch, we saw a truck and ran towards it, but only 1 boy from our group was quick enough to run to it and jump in. They helped him in but could not wait for anyone else because they would all have been killed. The shelling began again.

I was left in the field with 5 children I did not know. The eldest was a boy of 17 and the youngest was a little girl aged 7, but she looked much younger. I thought she was 4. Three other boys were between 9 and 13. I do not know exactly. We had almost no clothes and in the evening it began to rain. On the third day there was rain and snow. We had no warm clothes, we were hungry, and dug ourselves into the ground trying in some way to keep warm. That was how we spent the nights and, during the day, we crawled towards the village. We could not stand up because snipers were firing all the time. The fifth night we spent in a ditch very near the village, but were afraid to go in because there might be Russians there.

On the sixth morning I said we must go into the village, because otherwise we would die of cold and hunger. We went to the outermost house. When the woman saw us, she was horrified. She quickly brought us in, washed us, and gave us whatever clothes she could find to change nto. She gave us bread, but her house was cold. She took us to her neighbours and they gave us the help we really needed. Talking there, we discovered people had been unsuccessfully searching for us. Of course, those days had consequences for us. We were all ill for quite a long time afterwards.

The account of Daresh

(born 1967, daughter of Alpatu Abdulkerimova, lived with her mother in Argun)

As my sister has said, we were driving along in the truck, not suspecting anything, believing that the further we went from Argun, the safer we would be. That proved very far from the truth. Shrapnel from the shell that hit our truck wounded me in the arm and I lost consciousness. When I woke, I found I was lying on the ground and, on top of everything else, had been wounded in the leg by more shrapnel. I did my best to crawl further away from the truck, but again lost consciousness. I really do not remember much. I remember someone bandaging me, but do not even remember who. I needed treatment for a long time. The doctors thought they would have to amputate my arm but, thanks be to Allah, it did not come to that. I do still need another operation that can only be done under clinical conditions.

Testimony of Razet Emieva, who was in the refugee convoy on 29 October on Petropavlovskaya Highway, and was also present at exhumations at a federal burial site on 3 June 2000

On 3 June 2000, I was present at the opening of a burial site the federals had made on 1-2 November 1999, near where they fired on a refugee convoy on the Petropavlovskaya Highway, just round the bend before the village of Tolstoy-Yurt. We were tipped off that there would be exhumations on 2 June, not by the authorities but by other people who, like us, were looking for their loved ones massacred on 29 October during the bombardment of our convoy. We agreed to meet at 11 o'clock on 3 June and go together to the exhumation but were slightly late and, when we arrived, the exhumation was already under way. With me was Padam Abdulkerimova, her daughter and some of my female relatives. There were also male relatives of Ibrahim Saidov, whose body was found in the pit during the day. We were a little late and when we arrived the excavations were in full swing. An excavator was being used because digging by hand would have been impossible. The wheel of the truck we had been travelling in was already visible. I recognised it at once, because the 2 front wheels of our GAZ had tractor tyres. They pulled out our GAZ and continued excavating. When a woman's arm appeared, the lad operating the excavator stopped and they began digging by hand.

They dug very carefully. A head appeared, a white roll-neck sweater, and it became clear that this was the body of Zara Abdulkerimova. It was not decomposed but was beginning to deteriorate. All the limbs were in place.

The lad who had very carefully dug round and recovered the body of Zara, continued working just as carefully, not allowing others to rush things in order to to prevent damage to the body. A leg appeared in something **black, and the lad asked whether anyone was looking for** another woman. I said I had reason to believe this was my sister-in-law, Malika Emieva, although we were told she had been buried on 14 November. As none of us had been present, we could not confirm that. I explained that Malika was wearing black leggings, a black robe and red sweater, and that she had white hair. In due course we saw a black robe, then a red sweater, and then white hair. When the earth was cleaned off her face, we could see that this was indeed the body of Malika Emieva, my sister-in-law, whom we had believed buried long ago. The foot fell off her left leg, together with the sock, and her right arm was missing below the elbow. She evidently had a wound to the head as well, because the back of the skull fell off with her hair. I put it in a plastic bag and laid it beside the body. The people murdered were left in the car on that road, as they were when they died, for 3 days, and people who saw her in the car, said there was a woman with white hair and a damaged arm sitting in there. I know the shell hit the side to the rear of where they were sitting, so she was almost certainly wounded in the head. As I have said, they were side by side, Malika and Zara. Zara was also in the eighth or ninth month of pregnancy. Her body was recovered after 14.00 and Malika's body at 14.50.

Q: How do you know her body was recovered at 2.50?
A: The federal troops recorded it on tape. One of them was standing giving a commentary on all the excavating and recording it on tape.
Q: How many vehicles did they recover from this pit?
A: They pulled out 1 truck, the one we had been riding on, also a Samara the colour of wet asphalt, in which 7 people died, and also a red Lada. On the day of the exhumation they found 3 bodies from the Samara and earlier, on 14 November in Tolstoy-Yurt, they buried 4 other members of that family. In all, 7 family members were killed. I know that they were from Chervlennaya but do not know their surname. I remember the girl who was looking for them was called Malkan. Yes, and her father, whose body they found there that day, was called Sultan.

His daughter who died along with him was called Kuzhan. Two of her children were also murdered. Their daughter-in-law was killed, together with her 2 little daughters. She was breastfeeding a month-old baby girl. They found her little body too on 3 June in the same pit, and also the body of the 7-year-old daughter.

Q: What state were their bodies in?
A: They found the body of the baby as it had been, wrapped in swaddling clothes. It was just beginning to deteriorate, and the body of the 7-year-old was also starting to decompose. They found the body of Sultan, the girls' grandfather, on the morning of the second day, that is, on 4 June. But I am running ahead. After they recovered Malika's body, the next body was that of Ibrahim Saidov from Argun. His relatives were there and they identified him, but I did not see his body. They brought it and buried him here in Argun. After they recovered Ibrahim's body, they found the bodies of the little girls. Sultan's body and another corpse we covered with cloths so they would not be disturbed by dogs and left them until the next morning because it was late. Some of our belongings had been dumped in the pit too, although a lot had disappeared completely. We had had big bags full of our possessions: clothes, crockery, rugs and so on and we found no trace of them.

Testimony of Alpatu Abdulkerimova

(born 1932, lived in Argun)
When the shelling of Argun began, we decided to get as far away as possible from the bombs and shells in the truck of Kazbek Geraev, a resident of Kalinovskaya who was driving home. We had, of course, no idea what awaited us on the journey. By that time the fighting was already over in that area. On 29 October 1999 they were supposed to be providing a corridor for refugees from Grozny and Argun, or so they had been broadcasting for a whole week on all channels of the television and radio.

There were 4 of us travelling: my 3 daughters (Daresh, born 1967; Umani, born 1971; and Zara, born 1973) and myself. With us, we took all our possessions, money and gold jewellery. In total there were 28 of us in the truck.

Near Tolstoy-Yurt, our convoy came under fire. We were riding along peacefully, with white flags, suspecting nothing. Our truck took a sharp bend round a hill and was directly hit by an artillery shell. It happened after 9 o'clock in the morning, not far from Tolstoy-Yurt and Goryachevodsk. Climbing down from the truck, I saw Lena lying on the board upside down. I pulled her down, thinking she was dead: she was alive, but wounded. I noticed Daresh was injured, but could not help her because something hit my head and I lost consciousness. When I came to, I crawled as far as I could from the truck. When the second shell exploded, even more people were wounded. This shell was fired at another vehicle. For 4 and a half hours we were lying there and could not even raise our heads because of the shelling. We saw them destroying cars, vehicles burning, people dying. The vehicles were being shelled, by tanks or something else, I don't know, but not bombs or missiles. We did not have aircraft bombing us. I remember a family from Staraya Sunzha died, 5 people. The bodies were charred. Some of the local lads brought them in during the night in their Gazelle van. Aimani was also killed; she was from Vedeno and married to Nasuhanov of Argun. Her son was with her. He was aged about 20 and was wounded. He took his mother's body to Naur District.

Q: Tell me, no one could help you, so why did you stay there for such a long time?

A: It is certainly true that no one could help us. Not a single vehicle came from the direction of Tolstoy-Yurt. We heard later they were not allowed through to us. Any vehicles which came from Petropavlovskaya drove round the wrecked vehicles and themselves came under shellfire.

Q: How many vehicles were wrecked then?

A: I just cannot tell you exactly.

Q: Well, all the same, approximately.

A: Approximately, perhaps more than 30 vehicles. When I had counted 15, I could not go on. I was scared. I was just too scared. I could not even see all the vehicles because my view was blocked by cars, and smoke. And you could not just raise your head, because of the shooting. I saw 1 car burn. There were 12 wounded, 4 killed, and a fifth died 2 weeks later. She was an Uzbek, I do not know her surname, but her first name was Lena and she from Argun. We were travelling in the same truck. The Emievs died too: Hasan, Madina and Malika, a father and 2 daughters. My daughter was killed too, Zara Abdulkerimova. She was pregnant. A bit after 1 o'clock in the afternoon a vehicle with local lads approached from Tolstoy-Yurt. We shouted to them, „Go away, and they will shoot at you too. They called to us, „Anyone who can, run to the

truck. We are not leaving without you. We have come to collect you."

They jumped out of the truck and started collecting the dead and wounded and putting them in the car. They picked me up too. I knew immediately that my daughter Zara had been killed, but the snipers did not let them pick up her body. Zara's head was broken and her body had been mutilated by shrapnel. They were able to take my second daughter, Daresh, though, and gave her first aid in the car. They stopped her bleeding.

That not only saved her life, it saved her arm and leg too. They brought us in the crammed truck to the hospital in Tolstoy-Yurt where we were given the treatment we so needed.

We were not able to bury Zara at once. I asked one lad to go to the truck and throw her down to me but suddenly, out of nowhere, a shell exploded and we had to jump back. Fortunately, it did not hit us but exploded on the far side of the truck. We were not able to collect her body that day, and afterwards they did not allow anyone to go back there. Everyone who was left in the field that day they buried who knows where.

I was able to identify and bury my daughter only on 3 June, 7 months after she died. All that time I was running round their offices, asking them to give me my daughter's body to commit to the earth according to our customs. My daughter was carrying a baby in her womb in the eighth month of pregnancy. It was her first pregnancy. She died before she could experience the happiness of motherhood. We found out they were buried in the yard of an asphalt factory not far from the site of the massacre. They buried them along with the vehicles they were in in some kind of a big pit. In addition to our truck, there were another 3 cars buried there, badly mangled. I recognised our truck immediately, because it had tractor tyres. They told us no people were buried there, pretending it was only vehicles, but we did not listen to them. We insisted they should keep digging. They used an excavator, because it was impossible to dig a pit like that by hand. They had taken care to compact it. When they pulled out the truck I heard Daresh cry, „Careful! I can see Zara's head, that is her hair." My son began carefully digging round the head by hand and we saw her robe. It really was her. We carefully recovered her body. She was wearing the same clothes but there was nothing in the pockets, and none of the gold jewellery she had on her when we left: no heavy gold chain or earrings. Neither did we find the bag of money she had. All the household goods we had brought: a refrigerator, a washing machine, tables ... there was no sign of any of it, not even fragments of them in the pit.

After Zara, they dug up Malika Emieva's body. She was lying not far from Zara. They were both left that day in the car. They also dug up the bodies of 2 children, one a baby. They were from Chervlennaya.

After them, they found the remains of Ibrahim Saidov from Argun. His body was in a terrible state.

On the second morning they dug up the body of Sultan and 1 other man, but nobody could identify him. Later I heard he was from Tsatsan-

Yurt, but I do not know for sure. Sultan from Chervlennaya was the grandfather of the 2 girls exhumed on the evening of the third.

The Ozdamirov family

(a grandmother and 3 grandchildren who were in the refugee convoy on 29 October 1999)
Ozdamirova, Lena, born 15 September 1931; died 13 November 1999 from wounds inflicted on 29 October 1999;
Ozdamirov, Aslan, grandson of Lena;
Ozdamirov, Usman, grandson of Lena;
Shitaev, Adam, grandson of Lena;
Ozdamirov, Hanbatyr, husband of Lena;
Ozdamirova, Maiya, daughter of Lena, mother of Adam Shitaev

The account of Aslan Ozdamirov, 15

(born 15 November 1984, lived in Argun)
After we set off, I saw a flash in the distance, something hit our truck, and I jumped out. I quickly lay on the ground and saw the blast had thrown grandmother out. She was unconscious. Grandmother's name is Lena. When I looked up again, I saw a car explode. It was a Lada 99, and a fragment from the explosion hit me in the neck. (It almost hit my carotid artery.) I do not know how long I was unconscious or how long I lay there. Then somebody picked me up and carried me to a vehicle.

They were people from Tolstoy-Yurt.

We were taken to the hospital there. I was in a bed at the hospital for 2 days. I was told the fragment had just grazed my neck, They gave me an injection and put on a bandage. From the hospital we were sent to Mozdok, but did not go all the way there. Instead we were taken to the hospital in Znamenskoye. There they found I had a fragment in my neck which had almost hit the carotid artery. They gave me an operation and removed the splinter, which had come to rest in the back of my head. They put a collar on my neck. After the operation, they looked after me for 10 days.

The account of Usman Ozdamirov, 12

(born 19 May 1987)
When I jumped out of the truck, I saw grandmother. She was trying to get out of the car but the next explosion blew her out, hitting the side. A Lada 9 stopped behind our car but it was hit by a shell. There were people in it. Two were sitting in the front. The driver tried to crawl out of the car but could not. There were people in the back too. They were all killed. There was a boy about 8 years old in the car in front of us. His legs were blown off. It was like all the flesh had been cut off his bones.

His father was torn in half. The upper part of his body was thrown from the car. A 4-month-old baby was blasted out of the same car. It was covered in blood. Later he was found alive. Nothing had happened to him. They were the Saidov family.

Our driver, Kazbek, was injured too, and also our neighbour Emieva. Her whole face was covered in blood. Then I saw a Kamaz truck with a red cabin on fire. They said there were a woman and a child in it.

They were burned alive. Also a Gazelle van was on fire but the people managed to get out in time. They shot a motorbike too and it overturned.

A truck with cattle managed to get through. Another Gazelle van was left in that place in the field. We lay on the ground for a long time. It was very cold. Our clothes were not very warm. Suddenly, a vehicle drove up and they shouted to us to run to them. Someone shouted to those people to escape but they started collecting the dead and wounded. I was wounded in the leg. They collected everybody they could, and people who could move got in too and the men drove off with us.

When the truck started, the side of it was hit by bullets from a rifle or a machine gun. It took off fast, and we were brought to the hospital in Tolstoy-Yurt.

As we were driving, I saw a man on the road without a leg. His leg was lying by his shoulder and he was dead. There were pools of blood everywhere. That man was lying there, the half a person that was blown out of the Lada. Cars were driving over him because there was such a panic. There were arms lying around. One boy had had his head blown off. They said later he was his parents' only son. There was another head. Someone moved these heads under the motorbike.

When a sister tugged her brother, she found he was headless and fainted.

People were talking about it in the hospital. I did not know them, but they say they were from Severnyi State Farm in Naur District. People's belongings were scattered all over the road. There were even chickens and cows.

As far as I know, the people who were with us who died were the Emievs: their father who got shrapnel in his heart, and his 2 daughters. One was Madina and I do not remember the name of the other one. Another girl was killed, and her sister Umani was out in the open with other children for several days. One of them was my cousin, Adam.

Umani's sister who died was pregnant. They only recently found their bodies and buried them. People said all the gold jewellery had been taken off them. Malika Emieva had a gold chain round her neck and that was not found either.

My cousin Adam and the other children saw them dragging the vehicles and clearing everything away from there. They saw it from a hill where they were hiding for several days until they came to the village.

When they came to the village, my brother was all blue. For several days he had nothing to eat except some plants, and they drank rainwater.

It was raining during those days. It was very cold during those days, and they all got really cold. Adam could not even stand on his feet, and the rest of them could not stand on their feet either. There was a little girl about 4 years old with them. There were 6 of them: the boys about 10 and 12, and another boy who had his seventeenth birthday out there in the open. Adam told me about it. The boys were brothers and the little girl was their sister. Umani had a wound in her head, and Adam told me about that too. They hid in different trenches because soldiers were shooting all the time and they were afraid they would get hit.

On that day a shell hit a house in the village but did not explode. They told us about it at the hospital when they took us there. At the hospital they took a piece of shrapnel out of my leg. It hit the bone and ricocheted back, but stayed in my leg. I was lucky, though. It did not break the bone.

The account of Hanbatyr Ozdamirov

(born 1932, Lena's husband. He was not with the refugee convoy)
When they started bombing Argun, my wife said she would take the children and go to relatives in Naur. I agreed. They got ready for the trip, and decided to go on 29 October because there were announcements on radio and television that on that day there would be a corridor for

refugees to leave in all directions. Our neighbours the Emievs were also preparing to leave. Kazbek from Kalinovskaya took them in his truck because he was driving home in it. They set off on 29 October 1999 after 8.00 am.

I heard about what had happened on 3 November. I heard that 1 of my grandsons had been killed, a second was said to have been slightly injured, and my third grandson had disappeared. My wife had also been slightly injured. I did not even know my wife had died (she died from her injuries on 13 November 1999, and I heard about it only in December).

She was buried by my great-nephew at the Severnyi State Farm in Naur District. We were not allowed into Tolstoy-Yurt. They put up a checkpoint there and did not allow even women through. They said, „Do not come any closer or we will shoot!"

It was very hard to be all this time without news and to be worrying about all of them. I went completely grey in the course of the month.

The account of Adam Shitaev, 12

(born 24 November 1987)
When our truck drove round behind the hill, I realised a shell had hit the car in front. Our truck stopped, and it too was immediately hit by a shell. Aslanbek jumped down from the truck and I jumped down after him but could not stand up. I saw Umar. He was running away from the truck, and another woman, and I ran too. The shells kept exploding. I saw a lady running up the hill (Umani, who was 28), and I and 6 other children

93

(Mohamed and a little girl of about 4 and I cannot remember the names of the others) joined her.

All the time tank shells and snipers were firing. We went and hid in a trench, but no one came up behind us. After several hours the noise like died down and, looking up, we saw a truck loading up people from the field which drove back to the road leading to the village. We ran towards it but only 1 of us managed to get in. The 6 of us were left behind in this field. It was evening already but the shelling continued and we had to shelter from it. We hid in a trench or pit and spent the first night there. It rained. We had almost no clothes on, and I was the only one with shoes on my feet. All the others had no shoes: they were only wearing socks. (When we got in the truck, they all took their shoes off so as not to mark the blankets they were sitting on, and one of them, I think it was Mohamed, had only 1 sock on.) Even my shoes were soaked through. I had a hat, so I gave my hood to one of the boys.

The next morning, the eldest of us, Umar, I think, went to see what he could find as shelter, because it was impossible for us to stay where we were. He found another ditch and came back for us. We crawled on all fours because we could not stand up: snipers were firing all the time. We found a wild rose bush and ate some berries, but they only gave us upset stomachs. From our new hiding place, we saw soldiers in armored vehicles drive up to the place where the shooting had been and take away people's belongings. They hitched abandoned cars which were not too damaged to their armored personnel carriers and towed them away. We also saw the federal soldiers kill the cows that had been abandoned there. We could see everything down there was scattered about and lying there for 2 or 3 days. It was only on the fourth day they started clearing everything up.

We spent 5 days in the open. We slowly crept down the hill, but most of the time we were just hiding because they were shooting all the time. Once we had just moved to a different pit when a shell hit the one we had left. We always crawled on all fours. We had almost no strength to stand up. There was absolutely no food except for rose hips, and we drank rain water. One time I found a burdock root and ate it, but the others refused. They did not know you can eat it. In the evening at the end of the fifth day we came to the village, but were afraid to go in because there were APCs driving along the road and we thought there might be Russians in the village. We found a ditch on the outskirts and spent the night in it. In the morning we saw a boy come out on to the road and Umar called to him. He quickly came over to us and knew who we were when he saw us. They knew in the village that we had gone into the hills and were expecting us.

They wanted to take us to the hospital straight away, but a woman who came out of the gate of a house immediately took us in there. When the girl saw a puddle in the yard, she ran to it and began drinking. The women could hardly pull her away from it. They were crying. Some more women came. They washed us and rubbed our feet and hands and gave us food.

Then we were taken to the hospital and treated there for 2 or 3 days. They rubbed us, gave us injections for our colds, and medicine.

It was several days before we could get to our feet, and even now my legs sometimes ache a bit. After I got out of hospital a woman took me home and looked after me. She applied poultices to me and gave me medicine.

I was in a state of shock so I do not remember very much. I have even forgotten the names of the people who sheltered me. I only remember the names of the boys in that house: Rasambek and Rizwan, but I have forgotten the name of the lady who owned it.

The account of Maiya Ozdamirova

(who was not in the refugee convoy)

I heard what had happened on 1 November, but did not know which of them had survived, who had been killed, or who was missing. People said they had seen a boy in a red jacket. That was my nephew, but my son's jacket was black and red. On the same day, 1 November, we heard about the deaths of the Emievs: their father and 2 daughters. Then I heard my nephews were alive, my mum was slightly injured but otherwise all right, only they had not found my boy. I thought he had been killed and I would never see him again. People said that many people had been blown to pieces. Something terrible had been done. On 11 December my cousin came and asked me how things were there. I said, „They seem to think everybody is alive and well." (I had already been told my boy had been found. He had been in the area where they were shooting for 5 days. For 5 days they could not stand up and go down to the village.) My son and the other children had been under fire. They had been crawling around looking for safe places to hide. On the evening of the fifth day they went down to the village but, just like in the Second World War, they did not know who was there: the Germans or the Reds. They saw armored vehicles, so you see, for them, that meant the Russian army was there, just like the German army during the World War. Well, I ask myself, for 4 days children were crawling on the ground with snipers firing. There were no barriers there, no trees. Could people really not see through binoculars that these were children? For 5 days they could not stand up because they were being fired at with sniper rifles. They crawled to the village, starving, exhausted, terribly thirsty, and did not dare go into it for the shelter they so desperately needed because they were afraid the Russians would get their hands on them. That is how afraid of them they were. They ate grass, roots, drank rainwater. When they came down closer to the village there were no longer any craters or ditches and they dug hiding places with their hands, using a catapult Adam had with him. They dug a little hollow, hid themselves there and that was where they slept.

In the morning they decided they had no choice. They left their hiding place. Some women took them in, warmed and washed them, gave them something to eat and took them to the hospital in Tolstoy-Yurt. When the women were taking them into a house, the little girl who was with them rushed to a puddle and started drinking from it.

They had difficulty pulling her away. The women gave them milk to drink but they were immediately sick because their stomachs were so unused to food. They rubbed them with alcohol before taking them to the hospital. You need to understand what I want to say: „Look at this cruelty to children! People can say what they like, I will not believe the Russian troops did not see those were children crawling out on that hill." And not only that. After all this, they did not let anybody near that place for several days, and when they did, people found nothing there: not the bodies of their loved ones which had been left there, nor any of their possessions or livestock.

It was later, when they had come back, my nephew told me he had been wounded in the neck, literally millimeters from his carotid artery. He told me, „Detsi, I was not shocked when they put a dead body without its head next to me, but I was shocked when they put a body on the other side of me and the flesh had literally been sliced off it, and evidently in his death throes, his face had frozen in a smile. That did shock me." Imagine it! They laid a headless corpse next to him and he was not surprised he had to see and experience that! What kind of trauma must that have been for a child!

I think it was out of greed and nothing else that they made it so difficult for people to collect the bodies. When those people set out, they took with them all their possessions, their money and gold. The Russian soldiers did it out of sheer greed! They shot to pieces a convoy of 30 and more vehicles, even though each of them was flying a white flag. Many of them were in open trucks: women, children, old people with their possessions loaded and people sitting on them. It was completely obvious that these were not fighters but a convoy of refugees. It was such a brutal massacre. I only heard in December about my mother's death, and she died on 13 November 1999. Her name was Elena Taborovna Ozdamirova. She was Uzbek. Our family was international.

We never discriminated between people on the basis of their nationality; for us they were either good people or bad people. Can you imagine, I was not even at her funeral, let alone by her side when she needed me. And I am not the only person in that situation.

When the Russian troops entered Argun on 2 December, I was still in a state of shock and did not know who was alive and who was dead. I asked the soldiers if they knew who had fired on a convoy of refugees on the Petropavlovskaya Highway, and one of them (he had a fairly high rank) replied that they had done it. They were obeying orders. The first commandant of Argun was the commander who massacred the refugee convoy, no matter whose orders he was acting under. They created those convoys deliberately and then fired at them. They covered up this bombardment so completely they did not even allow people to bury their dead, just dumped everything that was left of the convoy in huge pits: the bodies, the vehicles, and all the belongings people had brought with them One of these pits was recently excavated and the Emievs found the body of their daughter. She was buried literally a few days ago, on 4 or 5 June 2000, I think. But many other people have not found their loved ones who went missing there on that day. So, there are other burial sites which have still not yet been excavated. There can be no justification for such savagery.

The Dalaev family

(8 of whom were in the refugee convoy)
Dalaev, Aslanbek, father, born 28 August 1958;
Dalaeva, Yaha, mother, born 10 March 1959;
Dalaev, Umar, son;
Dalaev, Usman, son;
Dalaev, Mahomed, son;
Dalaev, Umar-Ali, son;
Dalaeva, Halimat, daughter;
Chermyhanova, Aset, grandmother, born 1937.

The account of Umar Dalaev, 16

(born 2 December 1982)
We left Argun after 8.00 am. When we came to that fateful bend, we waited for the other vehicles to catch up and hung out a white flag on our vehicle to show that we were refugees. The cars started and we moved off. When we rounded a hill, the children shouted, „Look, that car is upside down!" Suddenly, our truck was hit by a shell. There was uproar, everybody yelling and screaming. I jumped out and helped my mother down. I saw Usman had taken our little sister in his arms. Then I saw my father dragging our grandmother along. Seeing my brothers running uphill, I chased after them. We saw this hill and decided that it would be safer up there, but it turned out the opposite was true. There were shells exploding there more and the shrapnel spread further. I decided we needed somewhere better to shelter and we crawled further up, found a crater in the ground and hid there. For a while, we sat it out but then planes appeared. Although they did not fire at us, we decided to go on further. Crawling from one pit to another we left where the firing was but could not find anywhere to hide because snipers were firing at us all the time. Probably a few hours later (I know now the exact time: it was after 1.00 in the afternoon), we saw a vehicle collecting people from the field and rushed towards it as fast as we could but only 1 of us made it there and that was Usman. They drove off with him, and 6 of us were left behind in the field, because the snipers began firing again and not letting us reach the vehicle. Umani was crying because she did not know what had happened to her mother and sisters.

I comforted her and we went back to looking for somewhere to shelter. We found a new trench and hid there. There was a shovel in it and I later took that with me. We found a wild rose and some hips, but you could not eat too many. We were thirsty and did not have any water. We spent the night in that trench, and in the morning I broke a branch off a bush for camouflage and went to look for another place, because the firing started again in the morning and it was too dangerous to stay in that trench. There was a shell crater not far away and I rested in it. I took a good look around and crawled on. I found a ditch that gave a good view, went back for the others, and crawled with them to the ditch. We spent the second night there. It rained in the night and it turned out there was a drainpipe in the ditch. Water gushed into the pipe and we all got soaked to the skin. We were really cold all night and could not stand up in the morning because we were shivering so much our legs gave way.

Some planes started firing at a tower, but they flew off after half an hour or so and we again started looking for somewhere to sleep. It was like that for another 2 days. I told Umani I would sleep for a time, and lay down to rest. I fell asleep almost immediately but woke up with a start. I jumped to my feet and looked about. There were women down on the road and I shouted to them. One woman heard me and started looking around but did not see me because I was too high up. They left and I said to the others, „Let's go after them." We started, but while we were going down the hill it got dark. We were afraid to go into the village because we had seen armored vehicles driving along the road and did not know whether there were Russians there. We found a ditch and decided to spend the night in it. As soon as it was morning (which turned out to be 3 November 1999), we came out of hiding and stumbled into the village, having decided we did not care how we died. My little sister did not have strength to walk and asked me to carry her, but I had barely the strength to walk myself, let alone carry her. That is how we got to the village. We saw a boy in the street and shouted to him. He ran to us and was very sorry not to have a camera to take a photo of us.

Another woman came then, and she too knew who we were. At this point my sister saw a puddle, ran over to it and began drinking from it.

We could hardly get her away from it. Some women took us home, washed us, rubbed our hands and feet with alcohol and gave us some alcohol to drink. Then they tried to feed us but we could not eat anything. It made us sick. We were taken to Tolstoy-Yurt hospital.

The account of Aslanbek Dalaev

(born 28 August 1958)

My family (7 of us plus my mother-in-law, so 8 in all) did indeed come under fire on 29 October 1999, when we were travelling with a refugee convoy from Argun to Kalinovskaya. Just before that, there had been announcements on radio and television that a corridor would be provided on 29 October 1999 for those wishing to leave areas where there was fighting, so we decided we would. We trusted the Russian government.

We were shelled by long-range artillery. We jumped out of the truck in which 4 families were travelling, and ran into a field. We lay flat on the ground. There was no cover.

The shelling was continuous. I saw a Lada Samara hit by a shell. That killed 2 women and a man. Emieva was screaming. She had been injured. Her father went to help her but was wounded in the heart. He died there, in the field. We were all in a state of shock and I do not remember a great deal.

Then a truck drove up with some lads who shouted to us and we ran to them. We were shouting at them and waving our arms, warning them to go away before they too were hit, but they did not leave. They jumped out of their vehicle and began collecting the dead and injured. All my children had run off in different directions and I could not find any of them. My mother-in-law was wounded and so was my wife. These lads, may Allah bless them, collected all the wounded, and those who were not themselves injured climbed into the truck. They also picked up bodies, as many as they could in the time, and took us to the Tolstoy-Yurt **hospital. There the wounded were attended to, and those who could not** be helped there were taken to Znamenskoye and Mozdok. Of the children, my second son, Usman, joined us but the other 4 spent 5 days in the open before people from Goryachevodsk brought them to us. They got themselves to the village on the sixth day.

Halimat Dalaeva, 7, tells her story

(born 26 June 1992)

Question: Hi! What's your name?
Answer: Halimat.
Q: And how old are you?
A: Seven.
Q: Do you go to school?
A: Yes, I'm in second grade.
Q: Tell me what you can remember about the day you were shot at.
A: I remember I was in some pits.
Q: Why in pits?
A: Some men were firing guns at us and I ran away.
Q: Who was with you, and why did you run away?
A: (Halimat is crying and does not reply.)
Q: Did you have anything to eat with you?
A: No, we didn't.
Q: Did you have any water?
A: No, we didn't have any water either.
Q: Were you thirsty?
A: Yes, very! On our way I found a bottle and Umani broke the neck off it and, when it rained, we gathered rainwater and everybody drank a little.

Q: And tell me what you said in the field when you were hungry?
A: That I would like to eat 10 cakes and drink 10 cups of tea.
Q: And were you able to eat them like you said?
A: No, I couldn't. (She bursts into tears again.)
Q: And who helped you?
A: Some ladies helped me.
Q: How did they help you?
A: They washed my hands and feet and rubbed them with spirit and even gave us some to drink. They gave us clothes and something to eat.
Q: Did you eat anything?
A: I couldn't. I was sick. Then they took us to the hospital. They listened to what I said, gave me some medicine, and did an injection.
Q. Were your legs hurting?
A: Yes, and they still do.

The account of Usman Dalaev, 15
(born 26 January 1984)
Q: What were you wearing. Did you have warm clothes on?
A: We were not wearing very warm clothes. We were sitting wrapped in blankets, and our shoes were somewhere else. We took them off because we were sitting on the things we were taking with us, and when we jumped down from the truck, we had no shoes on.
Q: So for several days you were in the open without any shoes?
A: Yes, we were all barefoot except for Adashka, I mean Adam, but his shoes all fell apart on his feet. So you can say we were all barefoot.
Q: You at least had socks on your feet, though?
A: Yes, we were wearing warm socks, only Umar-Ali lost one of his, so he was completely barefoot. We all had different clothing too. One person had a jacket, another a sweater, someone else was in a suit.
Q: Had you taken any property with you?
A: Yes, we took clothing, and some valuables from our business. It all went missing that day. We did not find anything.

The account of Mohammed Dalaev, 11
(born 13 March 1988)
Q: Tell me what you remember about that day, 29 October. What did you see?
A: Our convoy was shot at from long-range guns.
Q: And what sort of convoy were you in and where were you?
A: It was a convoy of refugees, and we were near a village called Tolstoy-Yurt (Doikar-Evl). They shot at us and a lot of people were killed.
Q: Did you saw dead and wounded people?
A: Yes, I did. There were a lot of dead bodies and wounded people.
They all looked different: one had no arms, another no legs, another had no head.

Q: What kind of vehicle were you riding in? And what other kinds of vehicles were there?
A: We were in a GAZ truck. There were Lada and Volga cars, Gazelle vans, and other Gaziks. There were a lot of smashed vehicles. I do not know exactly how many. I did not count them. I did not have time for that.
Q: And were any of the vehicles on fire?
A: Yes, and there were people in that car too.
Q: What did you do when all this happened?
A: I ran up the hill to hide. I had my brothers with me, my sister, and also a girl called Umani and a boy called Adam.
Q: Were you out in the open for a long time? Do you remember?
A: Yes, we were out there for 5 nights. On the sixth day we went to Goryachevodsk.
Q: Had you seen that village earlier? Why did you not go there straight away?
A: We were frightened because people were shooting all the time, and then we thought there would be army posts there, **and RUSSIANS IN THE VILLAGE.**
Q: Why were you afraid of Russians?
A: What do you mean, why? It was them shooting at us all the time, with their big guns and sniper rifles. They killed Malika Emieva. I saw them do it.
Q: What happened when you went to the village?
A: We were washed, fed, given clothes and taken to hospital. We were very dirty, had almost no clothes. We were hungry. We had almost nothing on our feet because we had taken our shoes off in the truck and our shoes were all left there in the truck.
Q: Did you have anything to eat during those days? What did you drink?
A: In all that time we ate rose hips, and one time, when it rained, we drank rainwater.

The account of Umar-Ali Dalaev, 10

(born 26 December 1989)
Q: Where were you on 29 October? Do you remember that day?
A: Yes, I remember it very well! I was in a convoy of refugees. We were wanting to go to Kalinovskaya but we were shot at on the Petropavlovskaya Highway. When they started firing at the convoy a shell hit our Gazik. I jumped out, grabbed my little sister's hand, and ran up the hill. My brothers Umar, Usman and Mahomed were with me, and also Umani and Adashka, I mean Adam. We hid in a big pit, but then realised it was dangerous. We ran higher up, found another pit and hid there. We spent that night there. In the morning Umar went to look for a different shelter because they were shooting again, very near where we were. He found a trench and took us there. We spent 5 days in the open.

Q: What did you eat there, because I don't think you had any food with you?

A: All we ate was rose hips because there were plenty of them there, but there was nothing else. It made our tummies hurt, and it made us thirsty.

Q: What were you wearing?

A: I had a jacket, and 1 wool sock on my foot because I lost the other one when I was running up the hill on the first day. It was very cold. One day, it started raining from evening and we were soaked to the skin, and freezing cold. That was the second day.

Q: What was the last night like?

A: Freezing. We were very cold.

Q: How were you treated by the people in the village you came to after all your wanderings?

A: They were very kind to us. They washed us, dressed us, gave us food to eat and then took us to the hospital. Thank you to all of them!

Testimonies recorded 6-7 June 2000 by a staff member of Memorial in Argun.

Russian Cadaverology

Russian beasts sell the internal organs of kidnapped Chechens

The Russian occupation group is rapidly developing a new type of business, trafficking in human organs. Chechen hostages became donors. The depravity of the acts committed by Russian sadists in Chechnya has long overshadowed the propaganda delights of Kremlin specialists who continue to dully tell boring stories about the threat of the "Chechen terrorism".

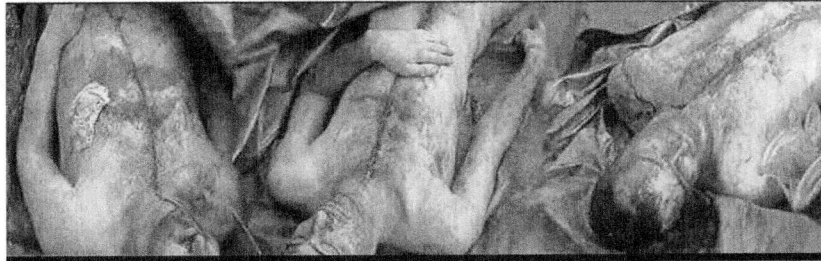

The recent findings near Khankala indicate that the "profitable business" is on a grand scale. They began to find corpses in the quarry on the road from Argun to Grozny relatively recently. However, the first findings confirmed the rumors that had been circulating in Chechnya for a long time about Russians cutting out the internal organs of people captured during punitive actions.

The first four corpses of Argun residents were found on March 27. There were no internal organs in all the bodies. Instead, they were stuffed with rags and bandages. All four Argun residents were taken to Khankala on March 11-13 for interrogation during the so-called "sweep".

Two days after the first finding, more than 35 bodies were found in the quarry. Most of them lacked kidneys and hearts. There were some corpses without livers and intestines and even more without any internal organs. According to some information, even though not yet confirmed, the mass grave was captured with a video camera.

It is clear today that the Russian occupation group has been using Chechen hostages as donors. Most of the bodies found belong to young people from 15 to 30 years of age. Only 3 out of 35 bodies are those of 40-50-year-old men. According to the Chechen party, a special group of military surgeons from Moscow operates in the location of the occupation group in Khankala, which has a special helicopter delivering freshly cut organs to Mozdok. According to the same data, the organs of hostages killed by Russian sadists are taken to Moscow, Saint Petersburg, and

Rostov. More and more information on the mechanism of the death conveyor has been received recently.

Having received an order for a human organ in Khankala, a team of doctors begins searching for a suitable "donor" among the hostages in the pits. Preference is given to "fresh donors", that is, to those who were brought to Khankala recently, still have unbruised insides, and did not get cold in the pit. The necessary tests are taken from a potential "donor". If there is no good "material", a corresponding order for a "healthy donor" is made to other Russian concentration camps. The "order" for transportation to Khankala is issued under the guise of "revealing another terrorist act and establishing the involvement of this person in murders and terrorist activities." The intelligence sources of the Chechen command also report that in some cases, the so-called "sweep" of a settlement is carried out specifically under the "order for a healthy donor". The punitive action of the occupying forces in Argun on March 11-13 also belongs to the "sweep under the order for a donor". The four hostages, Argun residents, whose bodies without internal organs were found on March 27, were 17-20 years old. The fate of 11 more hostages who were captured by the aggressors on the same day is still unknown.

From the moment of the very first "findings" of the bodies of young people with removed organs, who were detained at checkpoints and during the so-called "sweeps" in Chechnya and with following rumors about the bloody business of the Russian command, trafficking in hostage organs for transplantation, I have been kept my eyes on every such case. To be honest, as a doctor who knows the technology of providing and implementing the transplantation process, I treated such reports with great distrust at first.

Ali Merzho, Kavkaz Center,
April 3, 2001

Removal of internal organs from hostages in Chechnya

Certainly, not because I doubted that the moral qualities of the Russian leadership would prevent them from such barbarism. I thought it was impossible in Chechnya because of the technical difficulties of the organ removal and transplantation process.

But the irrefutable facts – bodies with removed organs – indicated that young people taken hostage by the Russian occupying forces, were undoubtedly subjected to medical removal of organs – probably for sale and transplantation – during their lifetime. I began to ask more and more questions.

The "route" of an organ from a donor to its recipient is a rather complex and time-consuming process, which includes a thorough examination of the donor with tissue compatibility tests, organ removal, preservation, transportation, and transplantation. Therefore, they need to have at least a medical institution with a hospital, medical staff, and a laboratory, not to mention other support services to remove and transport organs. It is incredibly difficult to hide such an institution in the basements of the destroyed Dzhokhar houses taken over by Chechen fighters at night. In this case, where is this institution and how is it possible to keep its activities secret?

In addition, it is known that Russian groups operating in Chechnya have little bloody wars between themselves because of less profitable "business". For example, in a dispute over control of oil pits or when dividing household goods looted from the homes of civilians, they have little bloody wars between themselves killing hundreds of their own people. Thanks to their greed, we become aware of secret incentive orders of the Russian command legitimizing crimes against civilians.

If this bloody "business" is not a myth, how do they preserve the secrecy over it? Why do institutions operating under top-secret conditions leave traces of their activities in the form of corpses with removed organs dropped near settlements and roads? Maybe one of the Russians wants to inform the Chechens about this terrible crime in such a way and provides these facts? After all, oddly enough, there are persons among this spawn that have not completely lost their human faces yet.

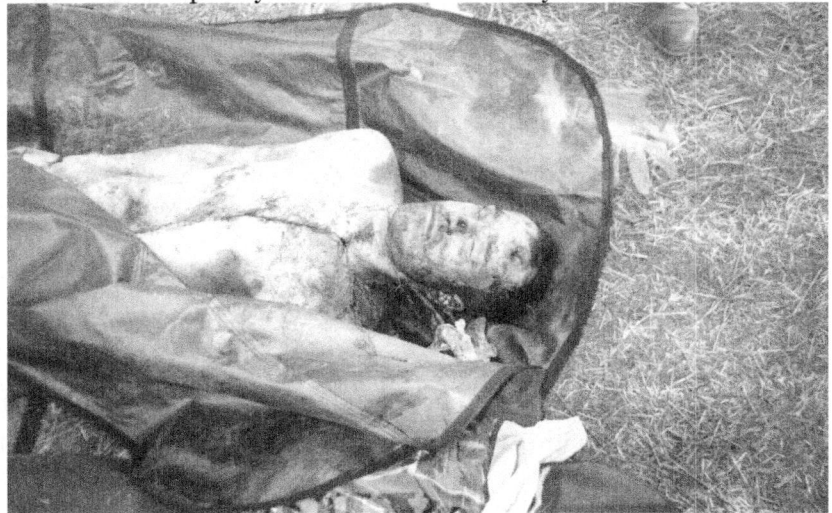

Ismail Musostovich Khutiev, born in 1982

If this is not the removal of organs for transplantation, why are organs so carefully cut out (mainly kidneys, liver, spleen, pancreas, heart, and lungs)? It is unlikely to explain all this only by the actions of ill Russian soldiers with sadistic impulses, although, as you know, there are many of them in Russian gangs in Chechnya.

Is not all this – the openly demonstrated facts of sadism in the form of lethal injections with poisons, disfigured and "gutted" corpses, heads cut off from bodies, and blowing up living people and corpses – done to distract us from a more heinous crime? In fact, why do they need these institutions to operate in Chechnya when mass hostage-takings and the removal of Chechens (who then disappear without a trace) from Chechnya are the usual and daily routine of the occupiers? Does it not mean that traces of the removal, sale, and transplantation of Chechen hostages' organs should be searched not only in Chechnya but also in Russian clinics controlled by special services?

In my search for answers to these questions, I had to contact many colleagues, both in Chechnya and in Russia, as well as collaborators since they had no reason to hide this information.

What did I notice when talking to my colleagues? They are terrified of being heard by someone else. They asked me not to specify their surnames and names. Chechen and Russian people have changed a lot. The fear of Stalin's times has returned to them. However, just like in those not-so-distant times, people try to remain human overcoming their fear as best they can.

Even the employees of the so-called "Ministry of Health" of the puppet Chechen administration do not hide that the removal of organs from hostages for transplantation is real. What really surprised and pleased me is that they have collected a lot of evidence proving these allegations, even though they do not have the courage to make them public. There are reasons for this.

It turns out that Chechen doctors received irrefutable evidence of the removal of organs from hostages back in early 2000 when they examined relatively whole corpses dropped by the occupiers near the roads with traces of surgical intervention, that is, they were cut up to remove internal organs from them. The doctors who examined the corpses claim that the wounds on the corpses are not the result of an autopsy as the Russian occupiers irresponsibly hurried to announce. It was a surgical opening of cavities of a living person.

Let me provide you with some excerpts from the conclusion of one of the corpse examination reports.

"...Judging by the areas of burns on the wound tissues specific to burns from an electric knife used by surgeons during operations to stop bleeding from blood vessels in the wound, it is clear that the wound in the abdominal area of the corpse is the result of a laparotomy performed when the person was still alive, possibly just before he died. In addition, there are areas of hemorrhages (hematomas) specific to a living tissue surgery on the parietal peritoneum, in the areas of the laparotomy wound, and in the liver projection. A segment of the inferior vena cava in the projection of the portal liver vein is resected, the distal and proximal ends of the inferior vena cava in the resected area are sewn up with a stapler while the remaining organs of the abdominal cavity and chest are cut out roughly and probably after the donor was killed. The organs are removed together. The vessels are not bandaged anywhere else. ...There is a pinpoint wound with hemorrhage under the skin (hematoma) in the area of the collarbone, on the right, which indicates catheterization of the subclavian vein for anesthesia during surgery..."

This enabled the doctors to conclude, "The corpse has traces of the lifetime liver removal by surgeons, possibly for transplantation." (Note that this was reported by a doctor who superficially examined the corpse. If there had been a forensic medical examination, they would have found a lot of other evidence of the lifetime liver removal and it would not have been difficult to confirm the authenticity of this and other doctors' conclusions during the exhumation of the corpse)

The doctors informed the relatives of the victims and the so-called Ministry of Health about the results of the examination. The doctors say that the "Minister of Health" of the puppet administration was afraid to cover these facts. It is obvious, of course, why they keep silent about these facts and one cannot blame anyone for this. There is a real danger that witnesses will disappear without a trace. But despite this, doctors believe the silence of these facts is tantamount to complicity in this grave crime against their people.

"The mass disfigurement of corpses of people killed after they were taken hostage at checkpoints and during "sweeps" cannot be explained only by the actions of single soldiers with sadistic impulses. This sadism is of a tailor-made and constitutive nature," the Chechen doctors say. The goals may be different, but the main goal, in their opinion, is to frighten the people, although they do not exclude that by doing so, they want to hide the traces of criminal business, trafficking in human organs.

I think it would be appropriate here to provide you with the opinion of a doctor who had contacts with doctors of Russian military units.

"The program of a psychotherapist who works in military units mainly consists of methods of psychological suggestion of sadistic impulses to a soldier," he says. "The psychotherapist instills into the soldier every day how good it is to kill Chechens by showing photos of disfigured corpses and saying, 'Look, if it weren't for you, a Russian soldier destroying these inhumans, we would lie in their place! Do not think you are killing a human, you are killing your enemy! Their children, women, and old people are your enemies, the enemies of your children and your country! Even their little beast wants to stick a knife in your back. Kill them and be happy that you have fewer enemies now!'

Then they show pictures of the human anatomical structure as though they offer to check the "correct arrangement of organs" in the corpses of these "inhumans". That is how they purposefully and methodically instill into a soldier the impulses of a sadistic killer."

In his opinion, the work of psychotherapists is aimed at hiding the traces of medical organ removal.

"First of all, after seeing a slashed corpse, a Russian sadistic killer trained by a psychotherapist, is unlikely to be interested in what it was slashed for.

Secondly, locals also confused by the mass disfigurement of corpses. They perceive it as a result of the sadism of Russian gangs."

"The traces of medical organ removal can be found on only 5-10% of corpses although the scale of trafficking in organs removed from Chechen hostages is huge," one of the employees of the Ministry of Health says. "The 'mystery' that shrouds this criminal business is not a mystery at all. However, as long as the country is driven by the FSB, no one will dare to seriously investigate the flagrant facts of this terrible crime against humanity. Pathologists and forensic experts controlled by the FSB will not issue any reports without its censorship and correction. The reliability of such conclusions raises deep doubts. Therefore, we have to limit ourselves to an external examination of the corpse, which is not always enough to prove the medical removal of organs."

"The 'unsubstantiated' Chechen accusations of the Russian military command of trafficking in human organs in Chechnya are beneficial to the FSB," the chief doctor of one of the Chechen hospitals says, "because the facts that have not been investigated are nothing more than rumors. Therefore, it is possible that the FSB periodically throws facts, corpses with removed organs mixed with victims of sadists and corpse rippers, into the lawless zone controlled by it where the result of the investigation of any crime is manageable and predictable. All this is being done so that the world gets used to the "unfounded and frivolous" Chechen accusations of the Russian army of trafficking in human organs from hostages. If the state recognizes its soldiers as ill sadists and actively helps to strengthen this opinion, more heinous and terrible things can be hidden behind it."

"The organs are removed from hostages not in Chechnya and not even in the republics and territories close to it, because it would quickly be revealed," one well-known collaborator believes. "Hostages are being taken to Moscow and Moscow region, that is, to the place where they will be least searched for and where there is more control over the objects in which they are being held. The fact that there are no living witnesses suggests that this operation is carried out by the FSB from beginning to end. It is their style not to leave any witnesses. For some reason, the corpses of some hostage donors with removed organs are brought back and thrown away at settlements and roads. I do not understand what for. Maybe so that the number of missing hostages is not very high. I suppose Putin is still thinking about the consequences. He guesses that he will be held responsible for it sooner or later. It will be more difficult to be held responsible for a missing hostage when there is evidence of his detention by state structures. The state, that is, Putin will be held responsible for him.

I really hope that I will be able to learn a lot about this terrible crime in the near future. Yes, I have my own view of the political structure of the republic, but unlike Kadyrov and his entourage, I am not an enemy of my people."

According to my Russian colleagues, more than 60 clinics and institutes in Russia and abroad use the "services" of hostage donors from Chechnya. There are 16 of them in Moscow alone. These lists also include clinics in Kazakhstan, Ukraine, and Belarus. The mention of the University Medical Center Freiburg (Germany) was sensational. It says a lot.

Donors are taken abroad alive. In their opinion, the ordered organ is taken in Moscow and Saint Petersburg and transported to anywhere in the world. It takes several hours, which makes it possible to deliver to a customer an organ suitable for transplantation. The customers have no idea that these organs belonged to hostages from Chechnya.

The institutions most frequently mentioned in this case include:

Russian Military Medical Academy of the Ministry of Defense of the Russian Federation (Saint Petersburg);

Main Military Hospital named after N.N. Burdenko of the Ministry of Defense of the Russian Federation;

Research Institute of Transplantation and Artificial Organs of the Ministry of Health of the Russian Federation;

Russian Scientific Center of Surgery of the Russian Academy of Medical Sciences;

Central Scientific Institute for X-Ray and Radiology of the Ministry of Health of the Russian Federation (Saint Petersburg);

Research Institute of Ambulance named after N.V. Sklifosovsky.

One of my Russian colleagues advised me to pay attention to one interesting fact.

The moment they started talking about corpses with removed organs in Chechnya, it turned out that Putin and the Duma pulled themselves together and took out the Law on Organ Transplantation from the archive to add two meaningless sentences.

One of them sounds like this, "at the same time, (during transplantation – author's note), the interests of a person should prevail over the interests of society or science."

Good words, there is no denying. According to my colleague, this was done intentionally. It was not for the sake of these two sentences that the media spent two whole months talking about "humane and important" additions to the law. This was propaganda against the facts of the terrible crime of the Russian authorities discovered by the Chechens. The propaganda was intended for the democratic West, which almost wept at Putin's humanity and immediately became deaf to the Chechens' complaints having heard these "right words". I doubt that the West does not understand that laws in Russia are written not only to violate them but also to hide a crime.

Russian doctors note the progress in transplantation centers, although in general, medicine continues to be poor as it has been so far. The number of organ transplantation operations has tripled compared to 1999. The prices of organ transplantation have been reduced by up to 50% in some centers. My colleagues found it difficult to explain the surge in such prosperity of Russian transplantation in conditions of general poverty, although they note that the criminal trafficking in human organs for transplantation is assuming alarming proportions in Russia.

Chechen doctors believe there is no wonder that Russian organ transplantation centers have revitalized their work. In their opinion, more than 30 thousand young Chechens who disappeared without a trace after being taken hostage by Russian troops have actually been taken to Russia. They are kept in special secret institutions controlled by the FSB and used as donors for the removal, sale, and transplantation of organs in Russian clinics.

I had a conversation with one of the Russian doctors involved in transplantation. When I asked if there were any changes in the Russian transplantation since the outbreak of the war in Chechnya, he answered, "Yes, of course. If earlier we had to wait for months for a donor organ, there is no problem with its delivery in the last two or three years. The only problem is the recipient's solvency. I will not be surprised at all if the president issues a decree on free organ transplantation to everyone who needs it. The special mafia will not lose from this. It will launder our budget money because the main customers for "suppliers of human organs" are not poor Russian institutions, but solvent foreign ones."

When I asked whether there were any Chechen citizens listed as donors, he refused to answer saying, "I am sorry, I cannot do that. It has to do with the fact that instead of the data of most donors, there is just a code in the accompanying documents of the organ, which corresponds to article 14 of the law prohibiting the disclosure of information on the donor. The notorious "dictatorship of the law" is all about this article. Even our compassionate patients who wanted to know who they owed for the saving organ out of gratitude, could not get this information. Some people even guess who they are, these donors under the code. I think you guessed it too.

Transplantation is one of the most profitable branches of medicine. One donor costs at least 200 thousand dollars and more. A disenfranchised and nameless living donor can be a source of great profit. Where there is a lot of money, there is everything – blood, death, and crime in law. We all understand that we are unwittingly becoming accomplices in the crime of our own mafia state. I hope this will not last long."

I remembered the crowds of distraught women in Chechnya with photos of their loved ones who had disappeared without a trace. These women hopefully welcomed European officials tearfully asking them for help to find their son, brother, or husband. I mentally addressed them.

"No one will hear our pleas, even those who survived thanks to your son's transplanted organ because our children are registered under numbers instead of surnames like in Nazi concentration camps!"

The religious world was horrified when doctors suggested cloning people and using their organs to treat patients. The condemning voice of Russian Patriarch Alexy II was the loudest one. Putin and the Duma quickly concocted a law that imposes a taboo on human cloning and using them as "spare parts". The most interesting thing is that Putin motivated the relevance of this law by the "ethical unacceptability of cloning for Russian society!!!" Does this mean that using Chechen hostages for organ trafficking is ethically acceptable for Putin's society and pleasing to the "God" of Patriarch Alexy II?

In this regard, I have a question for the institutions protecting fundamental human rights (UN, OSCE, PACE, and others), which supported the farce started by hostage organ dealers in the form of a "referendum" for Chechen donors. Do you really suggest that we vote unanimously and legalize Putin's business in Chechnya? If so, what is your share in this deal?

After Putin's visit to France, one of the Chechen journalists wrote, "The world is now convinced of the Russian president's addiction to 'transplantation' after he offered journalists services for the removal of one of the organs in Brussels. Europe pretended 'not to understand' it and recommended journalists not to tease him with Chechnya, which meant, 'Let him do anything as long as he does not get angry and talk nonsense.'

In fact, he was telling the truth. Indeed, Putin 'knows the places in Moscow' where suicide donors from Chechnya are kept to sell their organs for transplantation. Islamic fundamentalism has the same relation to this as 'Putin's society' has to ethics.

During Putin's last visit to France, Jacques Chirac's behavior demonstrated that he understood him well in Brussels. Knowing the guest's addiction to organ removal, he left him with the mayor of Paris and preferred to stay away. Journalists claim that the Russian 'transplantologist' did not understand the hint. Whatever it was, Europe with its games of silent pretense and hints may get to the point where organs with French, German, English, Italian, and other labels will appear on the shelves of 'Putin's donor organ bank' in the near future.

God is with us, the Chechens, we do not need pity. Europeans, I think it it time to think about your organs!" Chechens may not be enough after some time. It is your turn, Europeans!

Umar Khanbiyev
Minister of Health of the CRI,
Representative of the CRI in European Countries
March 10, 2003

Memorial Human Rights Center on the removal of internal organs from illegally arrested young Chechens

Three employees of the Ministry of Emergency Situations in the Ural car arrived in Prigorodnoe Village of Grozny (Rural) District on March 19, 2001. One of them told the local residents gathered around that there was an urgent need to bury the corpses of four men who were found in a holiday village near Khankala. About 20 people agreed to do this. The employees of the Ministry of Emergency Situations took the corpses to the cemetery, unloaded them there, and then immediately left the settlement.

Immediately after their departure, the road to the cemetery was blocked by the Russian troops. They arrived there in one IFV and several trucks. Refusing to answer questions and referring to the order, the troops did not let in people who wanted to take part in the burial of corpses.

However, several people went to the cemetery by another road. They took photo and video equipment with them. Before the corpses were put into the grave, the residents of Prigorodnoe photographed them and made a video.

There were autopsy marks from the neck to the pelvic area on the bodies of unknown people. In addition, two of them had incisions in the collarbone area and shoulder joints. According to the local residents who buried the bodies, the dead also had their brain cases opened (however, it cannot be seen in the photographs they took). The corpses were sewn up very roughly and negligently.

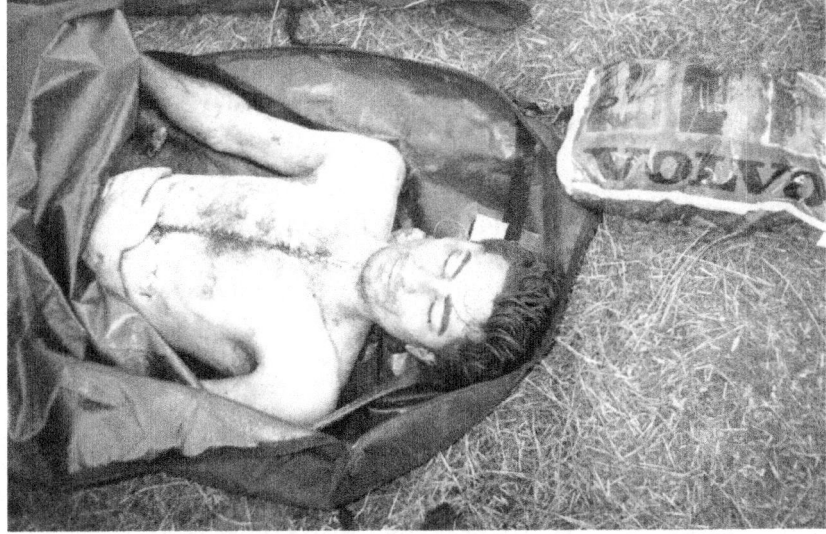

Muslim Umarovich Batsiev, born in 1976

Residents of Prigorodnoe noted that they had holes in the abdominal cavity apparently made with a special surgical instrument. There were no obvious signs of beatings and torture on the corpses, but they were completely naked.

The photos and video with the bodies were delivered to the Nazran office of the Memorial Human Rights Center on March 21.

The following people were identified as the dead on March 23 and 24:
1. Ismail Musostovich Khutiev, born in 1982;
2. Muslim Umarovich Batsiev, born in 1976;
3. Ayub Bibulatovich Gayrbekov, born in 1978;
4. Abdul-Malik Gazalievich Tovzarkhanov, born in 1963.

All of them were detained by the Russian troops during the "sweep" of Argun City on March 11-14 . Before the corpses were found, nothing was known about the whereabouts of these people despite numerous appeals to various authorities, including the prosecutor's office.

The relatives reburied the dead after a while. However, they did not want the second autopsy.

This tragic story was widely reported in Chechnya. It was like a visible confirmation of rumors that had been circulating long before that about Russian troops kidnapping people in order to remove their internal organs. To a great extent, this was explained by the questions that could easily arise and arose by any unbiased person after seeing the photographs of corpses and their video, which were widely distributed throughout the republic later. Here are just a few of them:
1. Where were the corpses taken to Prigorodnoe from?
2. Who performed their autopsy and why?
3. What was these people's cause of death?

Doctor Aleksandr Viktorovich Sokolov, the senior researcher at the Memorial Human Rights Center, analyzed the video in Moscow on April 10 to get answers to some of these questions. The following is its full text:

"On March 31, 2001, I conducted a preliminary analysis of the video received on March 29, 2001, from the office of the Memorial Human Rights Center in Nazran. This text is based on the results of this analysis and adapted for people without medical training.

According to the persons from whom the film was received, the video contains an external examination of the bodies and a scene of the burial of 4 people. They were detained during a "sweep" held on

March 11-14 in Argun and then killed. Their bodies were taken by the Ministry of Emergency Situations to the cemetery of Prigorodnoe Village.

It is important to note that the bodies of 38 murdered people found in Zdorovye Holiday Village in February and March 2001 were hastily buried in the cemetery of Prigorodnoe Village on March 10 before the process of identification by relatives was completed.

See the report by the Memorial Human Rights Center of March 11, 2001.

As I got to know later, some people in Chechnya began to claim that various organs were removed from the bodies and used for transplants. They also said that allegedly, there was a special mechanism for the export of human organs from the territory of the Chechen military base in Khankala.

The comment accompanying the entry corresponds to the above statement. At the same time, referring to the local doctors' opinion, the unknown author of the comment insists that the direction of the incisions on the corpses do not correspond to the traces left after the postmortem examination, since they were made in the opposite direction comparing to the usual one and that the facial expressions are too calm for the deceased.

When watching the video, we can conclude the following:

1. The video quality, duration, and lighting conditions are quite good. At the same time, there are practically no close-ups showing details of possible injuries on corpses. As a result, the reliability of the descriptions and conclusions set out below decreases. It should also be mentioned that the data obtained when viewing a photo or video material, are supplementary in nature compared to a direct examination in a usual situation.

2. The video shows the naked bodies of 4 dead men of different ages.

The bodies are preserved well, there is no obstacle to the identification of the deceased. As to the postmortem interval, it can be noted that there are no signs of mummification or significant traces of decomposition. At the same time, the traces of postmortem tissue changes are already visible on all the corpses. Thus, the postmortem interval may correspond to the dates indicated in the oral report if the corpse was placed under normal conditions.

3. There is a smooth round hole with brown-colored edges and surrounding skin in the collarbone area of the body lying in the row on the left (marked with A in the photo). Such staining may be the result of antiseptic treatment, and the hole roughly corresponds to the standard place where the subclavian catheter is inserted . At the same time, the appearance of such a hole may be the result of a gunshot wound, which was also treated. At the same time, the video quality does not enable us to draw an unequivocal conclusion. There are indistinct traces of two holes (mark B) in the right mesogastrium of the same body. These traces are similar to those that occur when inserting catheters for washing the abdominal cavity. At the same time, it is impossible to say whether an operation was performed on the abdominal organs because we cannot see the whole body in the video.

4. The general appearance and location of incisions on the corpses do not correspond to lifetime organ-preservation surgical manipulations and are specific to the sectional postmortem examination. At the same time, the direction of incisions in contrast to their location may depend on the personal habits of a person (often not a doctor, but a ward

attendant) producing the section and the access conditions to an autopsy table. The change in the facial expressions of the deceased is well known as smoothing of facial features and is described not only in medical books but also in fiction. It is explained by the postmortem spasmolysis of facial muscles and the beginning of the histolysis process.

5. Since there are no visible external injuries in the video that could be the cause of death, it is not possible to determine the cause of death. It can be assumed that some of the deceased were treated in a hospital. This also explains the visible traces of the postmortem examination.

The analyzed video does not contain any data in favor of the version of the organ removal for the purpose of subsequent transplantation."

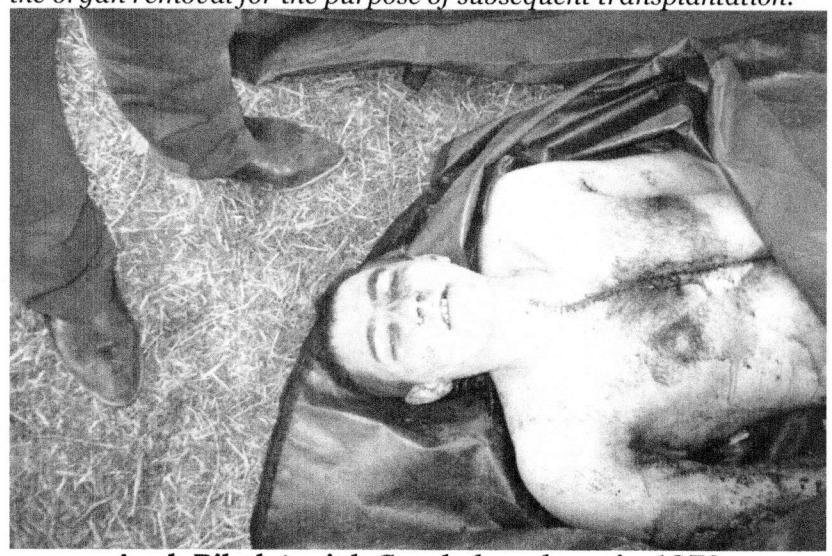

Ayub Bibulatovich Gayrbekov, born in 1978

However, this analysis has also raised new questions. In particular, it is known that incisions from the chin to the pubic symphysis are not made on a living person. But if the autopsy was performed by a pathologist, why were the corpses not marked and placed in a morgue or refrigerator until they were identified and handed over to their relatives? In addition, stating that "there are no visible external injuries that could be the cause of death" in the video, Aleksandr Sokolov expressed the opinion that some of the deceased could be "treated in a hospital."

The bodies had already been identified and even reburied by that time. Therefore, it was clear that this assumption does not correspond to reality, since Ayub Gayrbekov, Muslim Batsiev, Abdul-Malik Tovzarkhanov, and Ismail Khutiev were absolutely healthy when they were taken away from Argun by the Russian troops on March 12. It was exactly one week from the moment of their detention until their bodies were delivered to Prigorodnoe Village. Even though the doctor who examined the video writes "there are no signs of mummification or significant traces of decomposition" on the corpses, there are still traces of postmortem changes on them.

In other words, it follows from the analysis that if not all four, then some of these people died almost immediately after their detention by the Russian troops and their delivery to Khankala.

This was also confirmed by the subsequent events.

In May 2001, employees of the Memorial Human Rights Center met with an investigator of the Military Prosecutor's Office, who reported that on March 13, 2001, the servicemen saw the earth dug up in the drainage ditch while patrolling around the Russian military base in Khankala. Thinking that a ground bomb could be planted there, they called the sappers.

Instead of a ground bomb, four bodies were found there with gunshot wounds to the head from behind and in the back. They were exhumed in the presence of employees of the Military Prosecutor's Office, washed, and taken to the reception and processing station of the deceased of the United Group Alignment, which was also located there, in Khankala.

Upon the discovery of bodies showing signs of violent death, the Military Prosecutor's Office launched criminal case No. 14/33/0132-01. On March 14-16, the autopsy of the bodies was performed by seconded forensic experts of special medical laboratory 124 (Rostov-on-Don), after which the corpses were transferred for burial to the Ministry of Emergency Situations of the Chechen Republic on March 19. Thus, two burials were found near the main military base in just one month. It should be reminded that more than fifty bodies of the republic residents captured by employees of Russian law enforcement agencies, were found in a holiday village near Khankala in late February and early March.

Memorial Human Rights Center
February-March 2001

Russian cadaverology: "They are like Putin!"

The Chronicle of Hell photo exhibition, which demonstrated Russian aggression in Chechnya, was held on the eve of the Summer Olympics in London. The exhibition was organized by Sergey Melnikoff, the world-famous US photographer.

Two photographs depicting the half-buried bodies of Chechen soldiers killed in February 2000 during the operation of the Russian troops near Urus-Martan and Roshni-Chu Villages attracted the greatest interest of visitors.

They were perplexed about the half-buried bodies of Chechen fighters. Why did the Russian troops leave the bodies of Chechens in such an ugly state? Master Melnikoff replied, "This is a kind of intimidation action by the Russian troops."

However, Melnikoff was wrong. Half-buried bodies are "facing goods" put up for sale by Russian troops, a kind of butcher shop at the Russian military unit where they sell human flesh. Such an open jeering at the corpses of the deceased enemy simply could not be grasped by the master, who had seen and described a lot in this World. The reality turned out to be simpler and more monstrous...

Oleg Panfilov, director of the Center for Journalism in Extreme Situations, conducted a journalistic investigation called **The Story of Frank Hefling** in his book The Information Blockade of Chechnya, pp. 481-499.

You read and cannot believe it. We probably have not heard so many shameless lies spewed by high-ranking Russian officials since the Independent Investigation on NTV in connection with the attempted explosion of a house in Ryazan by FSB officers. However, if the explosions of houses in Russia found at least some resonance, the Story of Frank Hefling remained in the shadows...

So... In early March 2000, German television showed a film shot in Chechnya across the whole Europe proving that a real genocide of the Chechen people was taking place there. The three-hour film absolutely debunked the propaganda of the fight against terrorism in Chechnya raised on the Kremlin shield.

That is when high-ranking sycophants of all stripes rushed to save the image of Russia, whose only weapon turned out to be a lie in its climax.

Oleg Mironov, Human Rights Commissioner, "This TV story does not correspond to reality and is another propaganda step of the militants." (Interfax, February 25, 2000)

Aleksandr Zdanovich, Head of the Russian FSB Public Relations Center, "Any burials of persons held in pre-trial detention centers are out of the question because there is a strict and clear registration process for everyone entering and leaving the combat zone... The executions are a bluff. There are no executions at all. The enemy is destroyed in combat situations. If this is a captured prisoner, there were also no facts about the executions of prisoners." (Echo of Moscow, February 25, 2000)

Pavel Krasheninnikov, Chairman of the State Duma Legislation Committee, "There are no official confirmations or legal consequences of the shooting made by Western TV journalists yet." (Interfax, February 25, 2000)

Yuri Demin, Chief Military Prosecutor of the Russian Federation, "Every media report about illegal actions of Russian troops is carefully checked. However, as practice shows, the vast majority of such reports, especially those coming from Western media, is not confirmed after an inspection." (Interfax, February 25, 2000)

Sergey Ivanov, Secretary of the Security Council of the Russian Federation, "The video of the German journalist showing a mass grave in Chechnya is another fake of the militants." (Press conference on February 25, 2000)

Sergey Yastrzhembsky, Spokesperson of the President of the Russian Federation, "According to my information, this is a complete fake. ... What happened will be a good lesson for many Western politicians who blindly trust everything that is reported, and sometimes, as the case with the German TV company N-24 testifies, it is fabricated by the Western media." (Interfax, February 25, 2000)

And now... The "holy" truth of President Putin...

On March 6, President Putin gave an interview to the host of BBC Breakfast with Frost. Just by explaining his point of view on Hefling's story, Putin did not suspect that he thereby explains not only the reason for developing the Film special operation but also the technology of its discrediting.

D. Frost: ...the accusations of possible war crimes against civilians in that German film and, for instance, in today's Moscow Times. Do you think it is possible there have been any such war crimes committed by Russian troops or by contract soldiers?

V. Putin: ...We understand that one of the forms of struggle is information warfare. The video footage you mentioned, which had been shown to the world by German television, has now been refuted by our own media. Izvestia newspaper has carried information coming straight from the man who really shot those sequences and he accused his German colleague of falsification. In fact, the German journalist simply bought the tape off our cameraman and what it shows is the burial of rebels killed in action.

That was then presented to the international public as evidence of torture and execution of prisoners. Which had nothing to do with reality. This is nothing more and nothing less than a frontline of information warfare, of confrontation. I repeat, this is a complete lie and falsification.

In the end, Putin summarized what was happening around the film shot in Chechnya as "a complete lie and falsification." Now it is time to pierce high-ranking Russian liars with their own shit...

On March 2, 2000, the General Newspaper published a translation of the commentary accompanying the plot of the German TV company N-24, which caused a scandal.

"There is a farm field southwest of Grozny. The Russian army uses it for graves. Armored personnel carriers with corpses arrive one by one. The corpses are dragged across the arable land and put in shallow graves. The heads remain visible so that relatives can buy their loved ones from the Russians.

There is a grave aside, which is not like the others. This is presumably a mass grave of Chechen fighters who – as they want to assure us – were killed in battle. This explanation seems unreliable. The hands and feet of the bodies are thoroughly tied as it is usually done with arrested people. The bodies themselves are mutilated in such a way that it cannot be a consequence of military actions. Many men have their ears cut off. Is it a consequence of torture? May it be that these supposedly fallen fighters are actually Chechens who were dragged from Chernokozovo camp where they were simply executed?

The suspicion is well-justified. Even here, not far from the border with Chechnya, there are long lists of missing persons. All of them were arrested during the sweeps and have never been seen again. Only independent observers could find out their fate, but Moscow does not let them into the camp. Thus, there remains a terrible suspicion that the Kremlin is repeating Stalin's atrocities. A whole nation is on the death row list just like in 1944."

Alexey Slavin and Bakhtiyar Akhmedkhanov, the authors of the publication in the General Newspaper, pay attention to a significant factor, "At the same time, one significant detail remained outside the fierce debate of journalist Oleg Blotsky and his chief Kremlin lawyer Sergey Yastrzhembsky with enemy TV fabricators for some reason – THE FILM WAS SOLD TO THE GERMANS! Hook, line, and sinker as they say. It is at least unethical both from a professional and civil point of view to demand public satisfaction after that. Fundamentally, all this is pure hypocrisy in the light of other people's suffering and blood, which easily fits into the current information policy of the Kremlin." According to the General Newspaper, cameraman Blotsky was offering his shooting to various TV companies, primarily German ones, during that week.

On March 2, Radio Liberty interviewed Hendrik Niederhoff, an employee of the German broadcaster N-24, when it became known that Frank Hefling had been dismissed from the TV company.

- Mr. Niederhoff, could you tell us why your correspondent Frank Hefling was fired? Do you doubt the authenticity of the submitted video documents?

- First of all, we want to emphasize that we are not talking about a fake. The footage was authentic, and the Kremlin confirmed it. Correspondent Frank Hefling, however, made an unforgivable mistake. He claimed to have been present when it was filmed. That was not true. We were forced to fire Hefling indefinitely because we need to be confident in our correspondents. We need to know that they tell the truth and nothing but the truth. Mr. Hefling did not comply with this rule. We had no other choice. The reasons for this are arguable. Mr. Hefling faced a moral dilemma. He believed that this was the only way to draw attention to the situation in Chechnya, the only way to force the Kremlin to react, to force it to recognize the authenticity of these shots. That is what happened. Hefling knew that he would lose his job with his personal decision and pay dearly for it, but he was in such a moral position that he decided that he could only go this way. We as a station also reacted unequivocally. If we cannot be 100 percent sure that our journalists tell the truth in every detail, in every nuance, we have no other choice.

However, the footage itself, which was shown by many TV channels, is authentic!

Let us add that the German journalist lied because he was asked to do so by Oleg Blotsky. He took his colleague "out of the fire". He said that he was personally present at the shooting and paid a very high price for it. Frank Hefling did not know how mean Putin's journalists were.

After the international scandal subsided, a trial of the participants in that scandalous story miraculously took place in Russia six months later. However, this trial was inconspicuous, quiet. There was no public response to it.

By the decision of the Tver Court of the Central Administrative District of Moscow of October 16, 2000, the information contained in Izvestia newspaper No. 232 (25577) of December 09, 1999, in the article by O. Blotsky The Team without which I Cannot Live that "Colonel General Ivan Koroba, Head of the Rear of the Federal Border Service was dismissed for that deal", was found to be untrue. (Do not try to find this article on the Internet. The same "team" of Blotsky cleaned up the Internet so thoroughly that even Google Almighty turned out to be powerless – MT)

Okay, let us assume that the Russian court has punished two perpetrators of the international scandal. The punishment, of course, is inadequate, minimal, but okay... Were there only two criminals? How are those high-ranking officials punished – first of all, President Putin – who brazenly and publicly lied not only to Russians but also to the world community? Come on, ladies and gentlemen, who punishes the power-holders in Russia? They are promoted to high positions again and again. This is the mentality of the "dear Russians" who overwhelmingly elected Vladimir Putin to his second reign instead of putting him to Justice.

However, the miracles do not end there...

Just one year after this disgusting story, the International Relations publishing house publishes the book Vladimir Putin. Life Story. Who is its author? Sic! You will never believe it... The same Oleg Blotsky who sold the film to the Germans. This is truly difficult to explain why Putin entrusted his biography to such a deceitful and corrupt journalist, even if the latter was an FSB officer.

The first explanation for what happened is that only a "specialist" with the appropriate moral qualities can write the leader's special biography "honestly".

The second explanation is that the top officials of Russia are in cahoots with their pocket journalists free from all morality, who wipe their shit, who make their corrupt, bloody, and deceitful politics digestible. To put it in one phrase, "They are like Putin!"

There are many Chechen refugees in Europe, about 150 000. There are relatives of the murdered and tortured Chechens here, about whom Frank Hefling's film tells. Probably there are those who bought the corpses of their loved ones from Russian monsters.

As you can see, Oleg Blotsky, who sold the film to Frank Hefling, is safe and sound. Blotsky can testify in Court, unless, of course, he is promoted to the rank of "untouchables" by Putin's order as happened with Andrey Lugovoy, State Duma Officer.

Colonel-General Ivan Koroba, Head of the Rear of the Federal Border Service and seller of Chechen corpses, is alive. Do you recognize the lively corpse dealer in the picture?

If necessary, the International Court of Justice may request **the case of the Tver Court of the Central Administrative District of Moscow of October 16, 2000.**

The German channel N-24 has the original film. If not, we would be content with copies.

Sergey Melnikoff will be happy to provide the Court with the necessary high-resolution photos. And not only this!?!?

The International Court of Justice will not have to sort out much here, because EVERYTHING is already on the surface, almost all the nuances of the case have been revealed by Oleg Panfilov's journalistic investigation.

In short, a real opportunity has been created to the International Court of Justice.

Chechens in Europe, you have a moral responsibility to your tortured relatives. Do your duty. The Most High and the Highest Justice are calling

you for this! War crimes of mass genocide are imprescriptible, criminals must be punished, and there are plenty of professional lawyers in Europe! Strasbourg is just around the corner as well as the Hague...

Mayrbek Taramov
for the Free Speech website

PS. A letter from the Nazran office of Memorial to the editor of the website „Kavkazsky Vestnik"

The staff of the Memorial office in Nazran would like to know how you obtained the materials on the 29 October bombardment. These materials were collected by our staff as witness statements for a court application and were not posted on our website.

We very much regret that you have not been aware that the case in respect of the 29 October bombing is 1 of 6 cases already being considered by the Strasbourg Court. This is precisely why we did not publish these interviews, being concerned for the safety of the witnesses and wishing to avoid possible pressure on them (which could jeopardise the entire judicial process). Our aim is to prove in an international court that war crimes have been committed in Chechnya while ensuring, as far as possible, the safety of our applicants and witnesses.

Quite what your aims might be we are not entirely sure.

Memorial Human Rights Centre, 12 June 2003

Replies from Mayrbek Taramov to the Nazran branch of Memorial HRC

The materials in question were passed to me for publication by Ruslan Abdurzakov, CRI representative in Azerbaijan, back in autumn 2000. It would appear that, unlike you, one staff member of Memorial deemed it expedient to publicise as a matter of urgency the most atrocious crimes perpetrated in Chechnya by the military and political leaders of Russia.

These materials were published without delay in 6 issues of the *Caucasian Herald* newspaper in the period from 11 December 2000 to 15 March 2001, and subsequently 3 (!) times in the eponymous online edition. There are also individual witness statements by victims, and not only on our website.

I find it deeply regrettable that the Memorial Human Rights Centre has not seen fit as yet (and it is now 2004) to post the aforementioned materials on its website. (It was later found that the materials had been taken down from the Memorial site – *Ed.*). Clearly remaining silent about these world-shaking atrocities is very much in somebody's interests. One wonders how much more time you will need to consider, or what further large-scale act of villainy must be committed, before these materials are posted on the Memorial website and the juggernaut of

legal action begins to move? My aims, like the aims of any decent human being, are to speak and write about all the crimes of Russia's politicians and army, which I do. This is so obvious that it is undertaken by Chechen, Russian and foreign journalists and human rights activists.

Hushing up such crimes strikes me as no less evil, no matter how eloquent the clarion calls accompanying it.

According to your highly original logic we should remain silent about Russian crimes in Chechnya out of concern for the lives of the witnesses and victims. Am I right? In actual fact, in most cases that is exactly what happens: Chechens are killed and tortured but, with rare exceptions, even their relatives prefer to remain silent for fear of reprisals by the Russian army and their puppets. It is odd that you not only hold but even advocate such a point of view. In this case, as has many times been said, silence condones the crimes committed, which is just what is needed by the criminals in and out of uniform.

The European courts are hardly being bombarded with Chechen cases, of which there are currently no more than 100, as against 200,000 [people killed], and of these a paltry 6 cases have actually reached the stage of being considered. Even so, no one is putting pressure on the European Court of Human Rights in Strasbourg or holding it to account for this delay, although already 3 years have passed since these cases concerning monstrous and large-scale atrocities were submitted. By contrast, other cases of secondary importance submitted a mere 6 months ago have already been considered by the Court and verdicts delivered. For your information, many witnesses and victims who have filed suits with the Court are already outside the borders of Russia and have been given refugee status, which is what should be done for the rest.

This is what Memorial should be doing, quite apart from the other governmental and non-governmental refugee organisations. You should not be waiting „for a more favourable climate", because while you do the harsh climate of Russia will leave not a single Chechen alive, never mind the witnesses and victims.

Mayrbek Taramov, 21 June 2003

Facts Warning the World

Dissident Vladimir Bukovsky with Mayrbek Taramov's book Crimes of the Russian Century in Chechnya at the British Prime Minister's residence at 10 Downing Street

Nadezhda Banchik's Review of The Russian Crime of the Century in Chechnya by M. Taramov

I confess it was difficult for me to write a short review of M. Taramov's book, because I am not an outsider. I have known its author for a long time. Mayrbek Taramov is a fearless defender of his people. He is sincerely concerned about them and about Russia reeling under the Chekist terror. After all, we all come from the "Indestructible Union". In addition, I am Jewish and the words "Final Decision" (a phrase from the former title of the book) blow the ashes of Auschwitz and the darkness of Babi Yars on me. Indeed, the events described in the book by the testimony of eyewitnesses and victims resurrect the GULAG or even the gas chambers in my memory. However, how is a targeted missile shot at a maternity hospital more humane than a gas chamber? How is a cynically prepared targeted shelling of refugee convoys better than mass shootings in Babi Yars? How do the last words "Leave me alone, let me die!" shouted from the very depths of a tortured soul, differ from the last cries from a synagogue burned down together with the people locked up there?

I spent my best years as a PhD student in Moscow in the distant 1980s and the most terrible and the most bitter thing for me is what Moscow has become. It was once my beloved city that became for me a window into the world of high poetry, theater, and some unreachable heights of the genuine Russian intelligentsia... "Let's join our hands, my friends, in order not to perish one by one," we sang at the monument to Pushkin. The Okudzhava Union for us was not the same Soviet Union with its official friendship of peoples and stiffened silhouettes of old men in the Mausoleum... No, we did not idealize the dead desert surrounding us called the Soviet Union, we were a tiny oasis in it — an oasis of bright dreams and warm human relations where everyone's nationality was used only for mutual discoveries and mutual revelations, not for offensive nicknames and certainly not for any kind of discrimination. How happy and proud we were on August 21, 1991, when it seemed to us that our dreams materialized at the walls of the Moscow White House!

Alexander Men, Dmitry Kholodov, Vlad Listyev, Galina Starovoytova, Viktor Popkov (a philanthropist and a human rights activist who traveled to all the "hot spots" to save their residents. He became one of the first victims of the targeted destruction of philanthropists and human rights activists. He was shot at close range on his last trip to Chechnya in April 2001. Nowadays he is not even mentioned in the lists of those killed by the Chekist regime); Sergey Yushenkov, Yuri Shchekochikhin, Anna Politkovskaya, Natasha Estemirova, Stanislav Markelov, and Anastasia Baburova... All of them paid with their lives for that Okudzhava Union and for that dazzlingly sunny August day of 1991. For the honor of the Russian intelligentsia.

Some of them have left the fatherland, which has become an enemy; some have been overtaken by a terrible death far from this country, which one cannot grasp with the mind... There are still a few individuals of this human breed alive who continue to fight in this unequal battle and risk every moment of their lives. They oppose their own personality not protected by anyone and anything, with a naked soul, selflessly compassionate to every person, and not to the faceless mass the unpunished, to uncontrolled and boundless rampage of bloody violence. Mayrbek Taramov belongs to this breed. Devoid of "Herculean" features and weapons, they come forward against the almighty and heavily armed forces of evil in a whirlwind of slander and hatred inflated from the very top, from the very Kremlin that I once admired.

The country of my youth turned into a hostile state to me, because it declared war on my class, the intelligentsia. The swirling desert declared war on its last oasis. This is the true background of the bacchanalia of the "final decision on the Chechen issue, a demonstrative and shocking triumph of Dishonor that seized power." It turns out that I am not only Jewish, but I am also a German from the time of Hitler's Germany. I am hurt and ashamed for my Russian language, for Pushkin and Okudzhava, for my Moscow disfigured by the militant and mocking cynicism of the modern era...

I am a Jew from Ukraine, I am a Chechen and Russian at the same time and this unity in me is getting stronger with each terrorist attack, in which nationalities, classes, and ages die indiscriminately, just because they were accidentally unlucky to be at a certain point at a certain time... What is even more painful is to hear hypocritical condolences to the Russian authorities as if it was not they who established this bloody regime, as if they are the same innocent victims as those who died and suffered from the explosion. As if those responsible for the fate of the world do not know that a bloody trail of Lubyanka appears in all major terrorist attacks as soon as the dust from the explosions settles. As if the whole world does not know what needs to be done to stop this bacchanalia of murders and hypocritical farce on blood.

The book by Mayrbek Taramov breaches this nonsense. My blood runs cold to see what my compatriots are capable of! All right, Putin is safely hidden behind the Kremlin walls and behind the walls of his enormous wealth... Ordinary Russian guys are sent deliberately to act as executors at the same time and many do not disdain to "earn" a lot of money with this. What about ordinary Moscow, Saint Petersburg, Ryazan, and village residents who turn away from the terrible facts with stupid stubbornness and listen to self-deception unleashed on them from their TV sets? Can they really eat, sleep, and work peacefully after all this?

No! Every time facts come up showing that those who have tasted the unpunished bloody rampage on the "Chechen business trips" can no longer return to normal life. They carry the bacilli of violence sowing them all over Russia with riots, unreasonable shootings of civilians, and outbursts of groundless rage... The virus of the dirty war brought by immigrants from Lubyanka to the Caucasian land, returns to Russia by infecting entire generations, if not the entire people. It seems that the current Russian autocrats have already surpassed the Khmer Rouge and are inevitably approaching the level of the executor of all times and peoples, the bloody Stalin. Who will stop them? Who will save the hopelessly sick country from the epidemic of violence?! Another historical picture comes in my mind, that of 1917-1920. Red terror, white terror, they do not differ from each other. How long until this milestone for the bloody Russian train rushing back at full speed?!

The world of the Big Politics, the guardians of the Western democracy hooked on the Russian oil and gas pipes, do you really amuse yourself with illusions that you will shut yourself off from the increasingly brazen Russian lawlessness?! From the civil war that has once again engulfed Russia and no longer fits not only in tiny Chechnya, but also in the entire Caucasus? Do you really think you will buy off the Lubyanka predators who lost their minds from their enormous wealth that surged over them surpassing the wealth of all Arab sheikhs, with the Caucasus?! Do you think all this will not end with a senseless and merciless Russian revolt in

the era of nuclear weapons? Have you borrowed the reaction of ostriches to such events?
Read the book and draw your own conclusions...
Nadezhda Banchik, Journalist, Human Rights Activist, USA.

Recommendation of Elena Maglevannaya

I took part in the editing of Mayrbek Taramov's book, upon his request. Naturally, I read it from beginning to end. Here is my opinion:

Attempts to create documented annals of the events of the two Chechen wars have been undertaken before. However, in my opinion they have, in fact, been essentially spoiled by the authors' strivings to describe everything with so-called "objectivity" and without bias," i.e. as an impartial viewer. Most often this delusional "objectivity" resulted in a levelling, and in the hypocritical placement of the criminal and the victim on the same scale. That is to say, such authors placed the imperial Russian monster's aggression against the independent Chechen state on the same scale as the holy struggle of Chechens to defend their freedom.

What I liked very much in this book was that the author is himself a Chechen, one who does not shy away from naming things as they are – an occupation is an occupation and genocide is genocide – all without any reverence for the rival. Yes, the Chechen land, suffering from wars, needs peace unlike any other. But peace is not possible until those killed are avenged and the perpetrators of all the terrible events of these past years are named and brought to justice.

I also liked that this book is not written in the form of statistical data - the dead count, the scale of destruction, etc. Instead, it is written in the form of actual stories told by participants in and witnesses to the events that took place. As everyone knows, this makes a deeper impression on the reader. Naturally, the readers of the book will be regular people just like those described in it, and therefore it will be easy for them to imagine themselves in their stead. It will be easy for them to imagine what it would be like if war were to suddenly rush into their peaceful lives, destroying everything within an hour, and splitting life into two parts – before and after. Once they have pictured this, it will be easier for them to understand Chechens who grabbed their guns to protect themselves, their homes, and their families. It is simple and natural is it not? If an armed enemy that wanted to kill you and everyone dear to you appeared on your doorstep, would you not resist? And what does this have to do with all those fairy tales about 'international terrorism' fabricated by the Kremlin wizards?

This book truly makes a strong impression. When I, as a person who has not seen wars, was editing this book, I would have dreams of bombings and shootings. Everything is so clearly and vividly described in it that it seems as if it happening in front of you.

Thank you, Mayrbek, for this immense work, and of course, many thanks to all of those who were kind enough to share their stories. I can imagine how hard it was for them to recall their sufferings and live through them again. However, it is terribly important. We need such books so people far removed from war can look into its horrible abyss, become terrified, and perhaps look at the tragedy of the tiny nation of Chechnya from a different perspective.

Elena Maglevannaja - Journalist and human rights worker, Finland

Recommendation of David Kudikov

It was great joy that I learned of the publication of this book by renowned human rights worker, wonderful person, and my friend through correspondence – Mayrbek Taramov.

It is a very important and undoubtedly timely book, telling the truth about actual events in Russia at the turn of the 21st century. This is a truth that has been carefully concealed by Russian official propaganda. They have concealed it not only by the openly direct lie and by the lie of silence, i.e. the information blockade, but they also conceal it with obvious criminal-political acts.

These include the numerous murders of human rights workers and reporters like Paul Khlebnikov and Anna Politkovskaya. Safeguarding this lie is one of the reasons for the dirty bomb blast in 21st century London, a bomb that was not directly targeted at Alexander Litvenenko but meant also for him. The main goal of this terror act was to sow terror and force human rights workers, witnesses and reporters to remain silent about the crimes perpetrated by the Russian regime in Russia and abroad; to make them know that if they damaged the image of the Russian regime it would snuff them out anywhere.

The Caucasus is not just somewhere outside of Russia not affecting her future. Developments there concern every Russian citizen and will inevitably affect the country's destiny and future. Developments in the Caucasus will also make an imprint on the countries of the West who are pretending they do not see or understand what is occurring in Russia while sporting shiny smiles and shaking hands with those who commit crimes against humanity. REBOOT. Our grandchildren will have to swallow and suppress this. They will have to live with this in the future and pay for it. I recall a story told by Sasha Litvinenko. His work sent him to the Caucasus and a seventeen-year-old Chechen teenager was brought before him for questioning. To the question, "How did you become a rebel-fighter?" he received the following answer: "Everyone in my whole grade went to the mountains right after the graduation evening." Sasha understood that an entire class does not just take to banditry, rather, a whole class goes off to support a sacred cause – to defend the homeland, to protect their mothers, brothers, sisters, and loved ones...

The brilliant publicist and dedicated human rights worker, Mayrbek Taramov, has presented an amazing work to the reader. Any crime or wickedness dreads the light of truth...

This book - alongside such works as "Judgement in Moscow" by Vladimir Bukovski, Alexander Livinenko's books, the materials left behind after Anna Politkovskaya's death, and many other publications – is not merely evidence for the future court of history or testimony for judgement of the guilty, but it is also an appeal to the conscience of peoples...

President of the "Authors and Publicists International Association," writer, and academic David Kudikov

Conclusion

Russian television commentator Mikhail Leontiev on 22 October 1999 stated on ORT (Russian Public Television) that the attack with tactical missiles on the centre of Grozny was not in fact an act of barbarism, as it was being seen by the whole world. Indeed, in Leontiev's opinion, the news from Chechnya about the bombing and massacre of the civilian population was in fact tidings of joy because it would have the effect that „the Chechens will themselves bring us the heads of Basaev and Maskhadov and ask us what else they have to do to get the bombing stopped."

It is, of course, entirely possible that for Leontiev, Putin, Patrushev, Ivanov, Shamanov and other monsters news of the bombing and killing of the civilian population fills them with joy, but do the rest of the international community share their jubilation? To judge by their deafening silence, it would seem that they do.

Perhaps someone will accuse me of exaggerating. Not at all. I have merely tried to bring together scattered factual materials about the sickening crimes of Russia's political and military leaders. My conclusion regarding the conspiracy of silence of the major countries of the global community is well known, and my words are echoed by a heartfelt poem by Alla Dudaeva, the widow of the first President of Chechnya:

Hazy in the distance you see the forests rise,
You see a wending highway maybe leading to the skies.
Come close. Beneath the snowscape now see the filth and mud.
But yours is not my nation that is wading through the blood.

Not yours are all these buildings in which the stark holes yawn,
Not yours all the bereavements, the children we must mourn.
And yours is not the brother, just 18 years of age,
Dismembered by the Russians in the evil war they wage.

Not done in Chechen highlands yet, this war the Kremlin willed,
Not reached the norm for genocide, the Plan not yet fulfilled.
The bloodshed not sufficient even after all these years
Of Europe's conscience bathing in my nation's blood and tears.

Reviews

This book opened my eyes to events taking place in Chechnya, and the attitude of Caucasian countries towards Russia is now clearer to me... Material is wonderfully put together in this book. I recommend it for serious reading!
James Powell – Documentary photographer

To read this book through to the end you will need a very strong nervous system and an empty stomach... However, it is worth the read!.. What I shocked me most of all was that at the very same time as these events the whole world staked huge hopes on friendship with Russia. They were astonishedly listening to the Russian president's "harsh rhetoric," not understanding what he was capable of doing to another sovereign state. It is an honest work that should be made into a good film.
Dr. Ron Jon - History professor

This is one of the best documentary books . . . a living illustration of events in the Caucasus that up until now have not been very well known. I recommend it for reading in university Russian history courses.
Evelyn Barnard - Slavic Studies expert

Such documentary books are needed in order to understand the roots of political conflicts... Concealing such information is the same as hiding the cracks in the foundation of history by smearing them with paint.
Mattie Banks - Philosophy professor

This book shakes you to the depths of the soul, the scale of the tragedy as well as the warmth of the Chechen people, and the example of their mutual assistance and support during this great tragedy...
Patrick Newman - Independent journalist

Printed in Great Britain
by Amazon

18499008R00078